D0823529

Find answers to *all* your questions about today's hottest health issue in THE OAT BRAN WAY...

- How does oat bran work to lower cholesterol?
- Can you inherit high cholesterol?
- Just how accurate are cholesterol tests?
- Why are men more likely to have heart disease than women?
- What is a safe cholesterol range for children?
- Are "quick" oats the same as "instant" oats?
- Is oat bran the *only* food that could lower cholesterol?
- What's the difference between "good" and "bad" cholesterol?

... and much more.

Reach for good health— THE OAT BRAN WAY!

Most Berkley Books are available at special quantity dis-
counts for bulk purchases for sales promotions, premiums,
fund-raising, or educational use. Special books or book ex-
cerpts can also be created to fit specific needs.

For details, write or telephone Special Markets, The Berkley
Publishing Group, 200 Madison Avenue, New York, New
York 10016; (212) 951-8800.

THE OAT BRAN WAY

JOSLEEN WILSON

BERKLEY BOOKS, NEW YORK

This book deals with the important
relationship between diet and exercise;
in particular the positive effects which
oat bran has in lowering cholesterol
levels. The reader is encouraged to
consult with a physician before
beginning any new regimen of diet
and exercise. Responsibility for any
adverse effects or unforeseen
consequences resulting from the use of
the information contained herein is
expressly disclaimed.

THE OAT BRAN WAY

A Berkley Book/published by arrangement with
the author

PRINTING HISTORY
Berkley edition/April 1989

All rights reserved.
Copyright © 1989 by Josleen Wilson.
This book may not be reproduced in whole or in part,
by mimeograph or any other means, without permission.
For information address: The Berkley Publishing Group,
200 Madison Avenue, New York, N.Y. 10016.

ISBN: 0-425-11809-6

A BERKLEY BOOK ® TM 757,375
Berkley Books are published by
The Berkley Publishing Group,
200 Madison Avenue, New York, N.Y. 10016.
The name "BERKLEY" and the "B" logo
are trademarks belonging to Berkley Publishing Corporation.

PRINTED IN THE UNITED STATES OF AMERICA

10 9 8 7 6 5 4 3 2 1

Contents

Introduction
by Harold D. Itskovitz, M.D.   7

1   *The Cholesterol Story*   11

2   *Checking Your Cholesterol*   31

3   *How Weight Loss, Exercise, and*
Relaxation Affect Your Cholesterol   51

4   *Oat Bran Makes the Difference*   71

5   *Other Foods That*
Help Lower Cholesterol   87

6   *Supermarket Shopping*   103

7   *The Oat Bran Kitchen*   115

8   *The Oat Bran Way*   125

Afterword   157

Introduction

Cardiovascular disease has been our number one killer for a period of at least seventy-five years and is responsible presently for approximately 50 percent of all deaths in the United States. Three risk factors have been identified in our society that have a direct impact on the incidence of cardiovascular disease. These include high blood pressure, smoking, and elevated blood-cholesterol levels. In an attempt to reduce these risk factors, major national campaigns have been organized and have been in effect now for more than fifteen years. As a result, most individuals with high blood pressure have been recognized, and many are now in treatment programs. At long last, we are beginning to achieve a marked reduction in the number of smokers and opportunities to smoke in public places. Our problems with hypertension and smoking have not been solved, but we are well on our way. However, we are left to deal with what may be our most difficult problem, too much cholesterol.

Epidemiologic studies have been conducted among large population groups in the United States in which measurements of total blood cholesterol were correlated with frequency of coronary artery disease. It was found that at total blood-cholesterol levels of 200* and beyond (but not below 200) there existed a direct relationship between the cholesterol measurement and the incidence of coronary artery disease among adults past the age of twenty. In other words, the higher the cholesterol, the more likely one was to suffer a heart attack. Individuals with a total blood cholesterol of 220 had a chance of having a heart attack approximately 35 percent greater than individuals with a blood cholesterol of 200; those with a total blood cholesterol of 240 had a 70 percent greater chance of a heart attack. As a result of the correlations obtained in these studies, our adult population has been divided into three groups: those having a total blood cholesterol less than 200, who are considered to be in a desirable cholesterol group; those with total blood-cholesterol levels between 200 and 240, who are considered to be in the borderline high-cholesterol group; and those with total blood-cholesterol measurements greater than 240, considered to be in the high-blood-cholesterol, high-risk group. In the United States it is estimated that 50 percent of the adult population has total blood-cholesterol levels greater than 200, and 25 percent has total blood-cholesterol levels greater than 240. Thus, at least half of our adult population has an increased risk of heart attacks on the basis of cholesterol, and such individuals may derive potential benefits if their total blood-cholesterol levels are lowered. Unquestionably, something must be done, and a National Cholesterol Education Program has been organized to lead the war. The National Cholesterol Education Program coordinates private and public agencies to set policy, educate the public, design and conduct programs to help solve our cholesterol problem.

*Expressed as milligrams of cholesterol per deciliter of blood plasma.

Two general approaches have been undertaken. The first is a case-finding method and has as its goal the identification of people at risk, using widespread screening procedures to measure blood-cholesterol levels. Thereafter, efforts are to be made among those at risk to reduce blood-cholesterol levels by changes in life-style (diet) and the use of medications when appropriate. A second approach is to be of a more generalized nature, attempting to lower the average blood-cholesterol level in our entire population. It is believed that this can be accomplished best by improvement in health habits and changes of life-style, such as increased physical activity and proper food selection. The use of cholesterol-lowering drugs is not contemplated for the entire population, since the drugs themselves can have detrimental side effects and are expensive. Of the life-style changes we can undertake to lower blood cholesterol, the most effective is likely to be proper food selection. This requires a reduction in cholesterol intake as well as those precursor substances that can be synthesized by the body into cholesterol. Also, there are food elements (such as soluble fiber) that can help reduce blood-cholesterol levels by interfering with cholesterol absorption.

Science has taught us a great deal. We have learned from worldwide studies that societies ingesting foods that result in low levels of blood cholesterol have a low incidence of coronary artery disease and arteriosclerosis in general. We know that patients with heart disease can decrease their symptoms and risk of heart attack by using foods and drugs that lower blood cholesterol. We can now identify many of the foods that increase or decrease our blood cholesterol. In particular, the foods that can be helpful are those derived from fruits, vegetables, and grains especially rich in fiber.

No doubt, there is still much to learn. However, we have been provided with useful information to make a beginning. It is important to get that information to the public and put it into practice for our mutual benefit.

Harold D. Itskovitz, M.D.
Professor of Medicine
New York Medical College
Valhalla, New York

1

The Cholesterol Story

Cholesterol has been a "hot topic" for about ten years. Yet until very recently many people, including cardiologists, continued to believe that cholesterol was unimportant. It was "too confusing." What was all this stuff about "good cholesterol" and "bad cholesterol"? About some people who had one kind, but not the other? And did your diet really have anything to do with your cholesterol level, or were you just born that way? The whole subject became "controversial."

Fortunately, because of the new interest of the American public in health and fitness, the press picked up the cholesterol story very early and raised more questions. Thanks partly to their perseverance, and a group of major new scientific studies, the confusion over cholesterol has begun to clear up.

The central study that conclusively showed the positive effects of reducing cholesterol in the blood was the Lipid Research Council Coronary Primary Prevention Trial, which studied 3,800 middle-aged men with high cholesterol. The men were divided into two groups—one group received treatment for their high cholesterol and the other didn't. Overall, those whose cholesterol was lowered had 20 percent fewer fatal and nonfatal heart attacks. About one-fifth of the treatment group adhered strictly to their prescribed treatment; these men had almost a 50 percent reduction in their coronary heart disease risk.

Another hallmark study, the recently completed Helsinki Heart Trial, carried out over a period of eleven years, demonstrated a 34 percent reduction in heart attacks and death in a group of 2,051 Finnish men who lowered their cholesterol levels.

A University of Southern California study showed that by lowering cholesterol in 80 men who had previously undergone coronary bypass surgery the progress of atherosclerosis was halted in 61 percent and the coronary blockage was actually *reversed* in 16 percent.

These new studies are so important that the National Cholesterol Education Program has launched for the first time a major effort for professional and public education. In the last two years many of the scientific questions surrounding cholesterol have sorted themselves out. One critical problem remains —to find a relatively simple, uncomplicated way to thwart this dangerous health hazard.

While the link between high blood cholesterol and heart attacks has been well established, the connection between diet and heart disease has been less clear. Will reducing the amount of dietary fat and cholesterol that we consume in our diets actually reduce our risk of heart attack?

The objective of the hallmark studies described above was to determine if lowering blood cholesterol by any manner would reduce the incidence of coronary heart disease; these studies used drugs alone or a combination of drugs and diet to reduce cholesterol. The University of California study, for example, used a new drug, colestipol, in combination with large doses of niacin to bring down cholesterol levels. The Coronary Primary Prevention trials used cholestyramine, another drug frequently prescribed to bring down dangerously high cholesterol levels.

And the Finnish men were treated with the anticholesterol drug gemfibrozil.

The big question was, would it be possible to get the same concrete benefit—a reduction in cholesterol that led to fewer heart attacks and death—by diet alone?

A clear answer came in November 1988 when the preliminary results of a new study from the University of California–San Francisco showed that lifestyle changes alone, without drugs, could actually halt or reverse atherosclerosis in men with severe heart disease. Although so far there have been results reported for only 29 patients, the findings have far-reaching implications for the treatment of heart disease.

It is this kind of information that changes the way the medical community looks at the treatment of heart disease. It is extremely important to show conclusively that without drugs, just by changing your life-style, you can not only prevent the development of plaque in the arteries, but get coronary artery disease to regress. This new discovery is expected to have an impact on heart transplants, bypasses, and the other high-tech medical procedures that have become standard solutions to the widespread epidemic of heart disease in America. Studies like this one are expected to change the way physicians think—and their thinking is usually conservative when it comes to do-it-yourself cures—and get them to help their patients focus on behavioral changes rather than drug therapy.

As a result of these and similar studies, much new information—and misinformation—has started circulating about the way to go about lowering your cholesterol by diet. An effective cholesterol-lowering diet is often highly restrictive, and sticking with the diet over the long-term is difficult for many people. For example, a group of adolescents at a boarding school followed a cholesterol-lowering diet for eight weeks. Their average blood cholesterol fell from 178 (anything over 175 is considered high for teenagers) to a more acceptable 152. But when the students went home for spring break, they abandoned their diets, and returned to school with their cholesterol levels soaring above 180. Back under the school's supervision, their cholesterol levels dropped again to the safe 150 range. But during summer vacation the students again were free of supervision. When they came back to school for the new term in September, their average cholesterol level was 183.

In a similar study, 16 patients already experiencing angina pectoris—chest pains that are symptoms of fat-clogged coronary arteries—followed a closely supervised low-fat diet and exercise program and lowered their cholesterol levels from an average of 232 to 199. Once the study was over and they were no longer supervised, the angina patients went off their diets and cholesterol surged right back to its original levels.

Because so many people perceive changes in lifestyle and diet as difficult to adhere to, there has been a quest for magic foods that promise to lower cholesterol, regardless of one's life-style and regardless of the diet as a whole.

In 1984 Dr. James Anderson of the University of Kentucky reported that when his diabetic patients consumed three and a half ounces of oat bran a day their high blood-cholesterol levels fell 21 percent in three weeks.

Thus began one of the most phenomenal upheavals in the long history of cardiovascular disease. Is oat bran the magic elixir? Is it true that this common grain can dramatically lower cholesterol? What is responsible for its remarkable effect?

New questions have risen as fast as word has spread throughout the country. Does the form the oats come in make any difference, or will it work no matter what its source? Are the new products that seem to grow and multiply on your supermarket shelves as good as homemade? Will oat bran by itself do the job—or do you really need a total dietary make-over? Just how complicated is all of this? Will it save your life?

The purpose of this book is to answer the questions most commonly asked about heart disease, cholesterol, and diet—and specifically about oat bran.

Americans suffer 1.5 million heart attacks each year, and one-third of the victims die, making heart disease the nation's leading killer. Our defense against this epidemic has been dramatic intervention of heroic proportions—namely, bypass surgery and heart transplants—once the disease has progressed to the life-threatening stage. These methods of treatment require the ministrations of many skilled physicians, surgeons, and other medical people, along with enormous outlays of money. For the individual receiving the treatment, it means a long hospital stay and considerable suffering and wear and tear on the body.

And yet, unlike most cancers, heart disease is one killer that many of us can avoid simply by taking our lives in our own hands. First, we can identify among our population those who are at greatest risk for developing heart disease. Secondly, each of us has the means readily at hand to reduce that risk.

Researchers estimate that cholesterol, the fatty substance that can clog arteries, plays a role in 85 percent of America's 550,000 annual deaths resulting from coronary artery disease. They believe that lowering cholesterol levels in high-risk people could prevent as many as 300,000 heart attacks a year. Preventive cardiology is clearly an idea whose time has come.

The good news is that most people have a large degree of control over their cardiovascular health. For the past two decades the American Heart Association has been urging people to protect their hearts by giving up cigarette smoking, controlling hypertension, and lowering their cholesterol. Many Americans have responded to the first two recommendations. Now, increasingly, they are listening to the mounting evidence from scientists that if you lower cholesterol, you can prevent heart disease.

Some of us have gotten the message. The heart attack death rate in the United States has fallen roughly 3 percent a year since 1967. But that is a small dent in the massive statistics. In a national report released in July 1988, Surgeon General C. Everett Koop warned Americans that we are still consuming too much saturated fat and that our cholesterol counts are too high. Dr. Koop said that for the first time the Government had identified reduction of fat intake as the number one dietary priority of the nation.

According to the more than 50 nutrition scientists who wrote sections of the report and almost 200 who reviewed its contents, dietary fat—hamburgers, hot dogs, french fries, ice cream, and other common foods—still accounts for at least 37 percent of the calorie intake of most Americans, well above the 30 percent limit recommended by several health groups. A high intake of dietary fat, in the form of saturated fats and cholesterol, is linked to increased risk of coronary heart disease. A high intake of fat is also associated with increases in risk for obesity, some types of cancer, and diabetes.

Here are some of the most common questions and answers about the way in which high levels of fat and cholesterol in your diet can affect your heart.

Q: *What is the relationship between cholesterol and heart disease?*

A: When fatty deposits of cholesterol build up on the walls of arteries that feed the heart, coronary heart disease results. A heart attack occurs when one of these arteries is plugged and the heart muscle is starved for blood. Even though the heart muscle itself may be healthy, it will die when its supply of oxygen is cut off.

Q: *What is atherosclerosis?*

A: Atherosclerosis is a progressive disease of the arteries throughout the body. Excess fat and cholesterol cause plaque to build up along the interior walls of the arteries. As these sludgy deposits harden, the arteries become rigid, losing their ability to expand and contract. The arteries become increasingly narrow. This process is atherosclerosis, which leads to coronary artery disease. If the artery closes completely, which often happens if even a small clot forms, the result is a heart attack.

Q: *Exactly what is cholesterol?*

A: Cholesterol is a waxy, odorless substance present in every human being. It is one of a number of fats, also called lipids, found in the blood. Cells make some of their own cholesterol, but most cholesterol used by the body is made by the liver from raw materials supplied by fat in the diet.

Q: *Why is cholesterol dangerous?*

A: Cholesterol isn't necessarily dangerous. Pure cholesterol is a life-sustaining substance that plays an essential role in building cell membranes and sex hormones as well as aiding digestion. The body works to balance the amount of cholesterol in the bloodstream—manufacturing quantities of cholesterol to do the essential tasks, and eliminating the excess. When this balancing act goes wrong—either because the system malfunctions or because excess cholesterol overstrains the mechanism—a combination of cholesterol and fat, called plaque, builds up inside artery walls.

Q: *How many people in the United States have too much cholesterol in their blood?*

A: According to the National Heart, Lung and Blood Institute about 25 percent of Americans between the ages of 20 and 74 are believed to have high blood cholesterol, which translates into at least 40 million people who need further evaluation or possible treatment.

Q: *By how much do I have to lower my cholesterol in order to reduce my risk of heart disease?*

A: It appears that even lowering high cholesterol a little will improve your risk profile. Statistics indicate that a 1 percent reduction in cholesterol level will lead to a 2 percent reduction in the risk of heart attack. That means that a 5 percent reduction in cholesterol leads to a 10 percent reduction in risk. The National Institutes of Health advisory panel believes that with a combination of diet, drugs, and a reduction of other risk factors high-risk individuals can reduce their chance of having a heart attack by as much as 50 percent.

Q: *What is a safe level of cholesterol?*

A: For adults, a safe level of cholesterol in the blood is believed to be below 200 milligrams per deciliter (mg/dl) of blood.

Q: *I'm confused about the difference between saturated fat and cholesterol. Which one is bad for you?*

A: The body uses fat to manufacture cholesterol. Therefore, both saturated fat and cholesterol in the diet will drive up cholesterol in the blood. Originally, it was believed that foods containing cholesterol were the greatest culprits, but now we know that saturated fats—found in animal fat, butter and other dairy products, and tropical oils such as palm and coconut oil—are worse, in terms of boosting cholesterol in the blood, than cholesterol-dense foods such as eggs, caviar, and organ meats.

Q: *What's the difference between "good choles- terol" and "bad cholesterol"?*

A: The difference is in the way it travels in the body. Neither cholesterol nor dietary fat can dis- solve in the watery part of the blood. Thus, to move fat and cholesterol from the intestine to the liver and out to the cells, the body constantly wraps and rewraps fat-cholesterol globules in water-soluble proteins. The packages are called lipoproteins—*lipo-* being the prefix for lipid, or fat. The lipoproteins carry cholesterol to the ar- teries.

One group of particles carry cholesterol out of the liver and deliver it to cells throughout the body. This is low-density lipoprotein, or LDL. After the cells use the cholesterol, another group of particles cleans up the excess and returns it to the liver for disposal. This is high-density lipo- protein, or HDLs.

LDL is called "bad cholesterol" because an excess of them leads to the buildup of harmful deposits of cholesterol in the walls of the arter- ies. HDL is "good" because it is protective to the heart, cleansing the arteries and carrying fat and cholesterol out of the bloodstream.

Q: *What's the difference between cholesterol and* total *cholesterol?*

A: The terms *cholesterol* and *total cholesterol* are used interchangeably. Cholesterol is broken down into fractions determined by the lipopro- teins that carry it through the bloodstream. The major fractions are very-low-density lipoprotein (VLDL), low-density lipoprotein (LDL), and high-density lipoprotein (HDL). Several new subfractions have recently been discovered, but at the moment the three major groupings remain the most relevant when discussing cholesterol. When we say *cholesterol*, we are usually refer- ring to the total amount of all the cholesterol fractions in the blood.

Q: *Which is the more important component—LDL or HDL?*

A: The transport of cholesterol is a complex metabolic process whose intricate workings are not yet fully understood. We do know that when LDL and HDL are in balance, cholesterol does not damage arteries. When the balance is off, LDLs become trapped in the arteries causing buildup of plaque.

The LDL part of the story is clear: the lower the LDL, the lower the risk of heart disease. The facts about HDL are not as readily known, simply because significant clinical studies have not yet been carried out. Despite the lack of concrete evidence, however, many scientists now believe too little HDL is as important a factor as too much LDL. The higher the level of HDL, the more it may aid in counteracting the effects of the bad cholesterol.

New research indicates low levels of HDL can result in heart disease—even in individuals whose total cholesterol count is in the supposedly "safe" zone below 200. Therefore, it is becoming usual for LDL and HDL to be looked at in relationship to each other.

Q: *How does HDL get rid of cholesterol?*

A: How HDL works is not entirely clear. The flat, disklike particles, largely produced in the liver and the intestines, are like empty envelopes waiting to be filled. They scoop up the excess proteins, fats, and cholesterol, but how they return it to the liver for disposal is still a puzzle scientists are trying to solve.

Q: *What are VLDLs?*

A: VLDL, or very-low-density lipoprotein, plays a key role in the complex process of cholesterol exchange. However, the many intricacies of the mysterious substance are yet to be uncovered. VLDL is used by the liver to manufacture LDL.

The higher the level of VLDL, the more LDL that can be produced. VLDLs are often referred to as cholesterol "ferryboats"—capable of loading, carrying, and unloading packets of fat-cholesterol. Fat-cholesterol manufactured in the liver is loaded aboard the VLDLs, which carry them through the bloodstream to the cells.

Though individual cells can make their own cholesterol, they pick up additional supplies from the VLDLs. Special protein receptors on the surface of the cells reach out and grab cholesterol from the ferryboats. Somehow in the process of unloading their fats into body tissues the carriers ultimately become particles of LDL.

Some similar transformation may occur on the trip back to the liver—that is, HDL particles suck up the excess fat-cholesterol, transfer it to circulating VLDL ferryboats, which again metamorphose into LDLs that can be picked up and processed by the liver for disposal.

The process seems to go wrong when the cells become sated and begin to reject the VLDLs. Excess LDLs are turned loose, and continue to travel freely through the bloodstream, possibly catching onto invisible snags along the artery walls, catching other LDLs, and ultimately building up fatty deposits on the inside of the arteries.

Q: *Why do some people live into old age without a sign of heart disease, even though they pay no attention to their diet?*

A: Statistical studies with large groups of people have proved that diets high in animal fat can raise the amount of cholesterol in the blood. But some people seem to be immune from the problem. Scientists are turning to biochemistry to discover why a few people suffer heart attacks in their thirties and many more in their forties or fifties, while others reach their eighties and nineties without ever having a heart attack.

A cholesterol balance—or imbalance—can be an inherited trait. Possessing unusually high levels of HDLs, for example, may be an inherited trait that protects some people against heart disease, regardless of what they eat. Similarly, some people may be genetically inclined toward excess LDLs, which makes them vulnerable to heart disease even though they carefully watch their diet. However, a person's consumption of dietary fats can strongly influence cholesterol levels and is considered the first-line of defense against heart disease whether a person possesses a genetic risk factor or not.

Q: *How do you inherit high cholesterol?*
A: Biochemists and geneticists are finding a variety of genetic defects that may pervert the way lipoproteins handle fat and cholesterol.

For example, people with abnormally high levels of LDL tend to have badly clogged arteries and a high risk of heart attack. One inherited defect may cripple the liver cells' ability to remove LDL particles from the blood. In another inherited defect a protein attached to LDL disguises the lipoprotein so that the liver cells think it is beneficial and fail to dispose of it. In each case, the LDL particles back up in the bloodstream, some ultimately to be deposited in the walls of the arteries.

Q: *What are the other risk factors associated with heart disease?*
A: Heart disease runs in families. You are at greater risk if a parent, sibling, or other close relative had heart disease. The risk is even greater if the relative developed heart disease before age fifty. Other major risk factors are age—the older you are, the greater the risk of heart disease and heart attack; smoking; obesity; high blood pressure; diabetes; and being male.

Q: *How can I tell if I'm likely to have high cholesterol?*

A: The more risk factors you have clustering together, the greater the likelihood that you will
have high cholesterol.

Q: *I've heard that women today are just as likely to
develop heart disease as men. Is this true?*

A: Epidemiological data shows that men are still at
much higher risk of developing heart disease
than women, although in recent years the gap
has been narrowing due to several factors—increased cigarette smoking among women; birth
control pills, which alter a woman's protective
hormonal balance; and stress are believed to be
behind the rise in heart disease statistics for
women.

Q: *How does diet affect cholesterol?*

A: The way the body uses cholesterol can be upset
by excess fats in the diet. A high-fat diet floods
the bloodstream with fatty particles; the liver has
to work overtime to mop up the excess, and the
surfeit of fat-cholesterol particles then begins
circulating freely through the body. Unless it is
stopped, the excess fat begins to collect in the
arteries and leads to the formation of deadly
plaque.

Q: *Just what are triglycerides, and why are they
important?*

A: Triglycerides are another blood fat used by cells
for energy or stored for future use. These fats are
somewhat different from cholesterol, and the
role they play in the development of heart disease is not clearly understood. It is generally
agreed that there is an association between elevated triglycerides and elevated cholesterol. At
Baylor College of Medicine in Houston, Dr. An-
tonio Gotto, Jr., discovered that virtually all of
his heart-bypass patients had slightly higher

levels of triglycerides and lower levels of protective HDL than people without heart disease. It is possible that triglycerides may destroy the beneficial HDL. It is theorized that excess triglycerides may somehow label the beneficial HDL particles for elimination by the liver.

Q: *Which is more important—high HDL or low LDL?*

A: No one knows yet because the way HDLs work in the blood is not clear. There is ample evidence that raising HDL levels improves cardiovascular health; high levels of HDL may be able to reverse the buildup of plaque by pulling cholesterol out of artery walls. But it's also possible that HDLs are not really active at all. One theory has it that the presence of HDLs may simply signal the fact that fat and cholesterol are being cleaned out through some other means. So, as yet, the information on HDL is by no means conclusive.

Dr. David Blankenhorn's study at the University of Southern California, in which the progress of atherosclerosis was reversed by using drugs to lower cholesterol, indicated that the greatest benefit was derived from decreased LDL. Lower levels of triglycerides also appeared to play an important role. In his treatment and follow-up of 80 men who had undergone coronary-bypass surgery, LDL went down 43 percent and triglycerides went down 22 percent, while HDL levels increased only 37 percent. The process of atherosclerosis was halted in 61 percent of the patients, and reversed in 16 percent.

In the third world, where relatively little saturated fat and cholesterol are consumed, most people seem to be protected from heart disease by low LDL levels. Until more information is accumulated about HDL, anticholesterol therapy is aimed at lowering LDL and raising HDL.

Q: *Is it possible to selectively lower LDL and raise HDL?*

A: It sounds implausible but, in fact, you may be able to reduce "bad cholesterol" and selectively raise "good cholesterol." Diet seems to be the most effective way to lower LDL. Until recently, regular aerobic exercise was thought to elevate HDL cholesterol levels. (See Chapter 3.) Oat bran in the diet also appears to selectively lower LDL and raise HDL.

Q: *Is it true that there is a new form of cholesterol that is even more dangerous than LDL?*

A: Another form of cholesterol has recently been identified that apparently increases risk of heart disease. It is call lipoprotein (a) or simple Lp (a). It was spotted 25 years ago, but new information about the biochemical processes of cholesterol at work in the bloodstream has made Lp (a) the focus of a new strategy to understand atherosclerosis.

    Researchers believe that people who have a good deal of the Lp (a) type of cholesterol run double the heart-attack risk of people with low Lp (a)—even if their total cholesterol levels are low. If both Lp (a) and total cholesterol are high, the risk quintuples. The tendency to produce dangerous levels of this variety of cholesterol is inherited.

Q: *What is special about Lp (a)?*

A: Close scrutiny of Lp (a) revealed that it was identical to LDL with an extra protein—protein (a)—wrapped around it. The extra protein lets LDL masquerade as a beneficial protein called plasminogen, which the body uses to dissolve blood clots. Thinking that Lp (a) is plasminogen, the body, working to dissolve blood clots in damaged arteries, mistakenly grabs protein (a) instead, pulling its bag of fat and cholesterol into the artery wall. This creates plaque, which damages the artery wall. A vicious cycle begins as more and more of the disguised Lp (a) is drawn into the damaged area, supposedly for clot-dissolving repair purposes. In fact, the impostor protein creates even more damage.

Q: *How can I tell if I have Lp (a)?*

A: Researchers believe that of all the forms of cholesterol, Lp (a) may be the most common. Estimates are that 25 percent of the general population has enough Lp (a) in the bloodstream to put them at risk of heart disease. As of now there is no easy test to measure Lp (a). It is assumed that if you have a high level of LDL, you may have high Lp (a) as well.

Q: *I've been hearing about a lot of other funny-sounding proteins that are supposed to be better indicators of heart-disease risk than cholesterol levels. What are these?*

A: You are probably thinking of the apoliopoproteins. After the major fractions of cholesterol were identified, it became clear that many more substances were involved in the cholesterol balancing act than had ever been considered before.

A protein called Apo A-1 (apoliopoprotein A-1), for example, has been found to attach itself to HDL and help seek out excess fat. Apo A-1 apparently takes used cholesterol out of the body's cells, wraps it up, and carries it back to the liver for disposal. By contrast, Apo Bs are proteins that keep company with bad cholesterol. You will be hearing a lot more about these apoliopoproteins as their impact on heart disease is sorted out in research labs over the next decade. Understanding these proteins may provide the necessary clues to unraveling the many mysteries of atherosclerosis.

Q: *What is HDL-2?*

A: One very interesting area is the investigation of

the subfractions of HDL. As of now, two subfractions have been identified—HDL-2 and HDL-3. These components are still difficult to measure, but HDL-2 is clearly a cholesterol savior. HDL-2 is the component of HDL that seems to increase significantly in people who run or carry out regular aerobic exercise. It is also significantly higher in the blood of women. HDL-3 tends to increase with the consumption of alcoholic beverages, but it is still unclear whether it has any bearing on cardiovascular disease. For now, the subfractions are intense areas of investigation. However, total HDL cholesterol, rather than its subfractions, is still considered the important factor when it comes to evaluating risk.

Q: *What foods contain "good cholesterol"?*
A: "Good cholesterol"—meaning artery-cleansing HDL—is not found in any food and cannot be acquired by eating it. HDL cholesterol is made by the body and is found only in the blood. However, certain foods can increase the amount the body produces. And certain foods may also help cleanse fat-clogged arteries. (See Chapters 4 and 5.)

Q: *How do sugar and caffeine affect cholesterol levels?*
A: Although there is much speculation, there is no certainty that sugar or caffeine has any effect on cholesterol blood levels. Some studies, for example, suggest that refined sugars can make HDL levels fall. Others have shown variable associations with increased blood lipid levels. The Surgeon General's Report on Nutrition and Health concludes that the present evidence is too weak to assume that eliminating these substances from your diet will reduce cholesterol levels.

Q: *I've heard that alcohol will lower my cholesterol level. Is this true?*

A: It appears to be true. Several studies have shown that moderate amounts of alcohol increase the good HDL. However, no one has recommended alcohol consumption as an appropriate way in which to control cholesterol in the blood. Further, it has recently been discovered that alcohol increases only a subfraction of HDL, and that subfraction (called HDL-3) may have no bearing on heart disease. But people who drink modest amounts of alcohol should not have to worry that they are elevating their cholesterol levels.

Q: *I've been trying to quit smoking because I know it's bad for my heart, but I haven't been very successful. Is smoking making my cholesterol level high?*

A: It is not known how, or even if, cigarette smoking affects the way the body processes cholesterol. It is very well-known, however, that smoking is one of the three major risk factors for heart disease. Smokers have a 70 percent higher mortality rate from coronary heart disease than nonsmokers; in fact, the Surgeon General has estimated that cigarette smoking is responsible for approximately 30 percent of all deaths from coronary heart disease in the United States each year.

Smoking, high blood pressure, and high cholesterol seem to act synergistically. That is, the deadly effect of the group together is greater than the sum of its parts. Therefore, if you continue to smoke, you must be constantly vigilant not to aggravate other risk factors, such as high cholesterol.

Q: *I am a smoker. My doctor says my cholesterol level is normal, but she says I should quit smoking anyway. Why?*

A: A normal cholesterol level cannot protect your heart from the damaging effects of cigarette smoking. Again, risk factors interact with each other—the more risk factors you have clustering together, the worse the overall impact will be on your heart. Eliminating even one risk factor vastly improves the outlook.

Q: *How does being overweight contribute to increased cholesterol?*

A: Thinness and fatness does not necessarily correlate with cholesterol. You can be bone thin and still have high levels of blood cholesterol. At the same time, people who are overweight are more likely to develop heart disease as well as other diseases.

In the past, doctors were concerned about obesity because it seemed to go along with other conditions. Today, however, researchers are paying increasing attention to obesity as an independent risk factor for coronary heart disease. One of the things they've discovered is that fat itself may not be as important as its location in the body. The Honolulu Heart Program, which involved 7,692 men, showed that the way the weight was distributed was more significant than total body mass. Men whose weight was concentrated around the chest and upper torso had a much greater risk of heart disease than men whose weight was evenly distributed or men who were "pear-shaped."

Q: *Is it true that a person's cholesterol levels change with the seasons?*

Q: Strangely enough, cholesterol levels do appear to change with the seasons. A team of federally sponsored researchers measured cholesterol levels periodically for four years in more than 1,400 middle-aged men in the course of a major research project. The men, all of whom had high cholesterol levels, were in an untreated control group. An analysis of all the findings turned up the interesting fact that the average cholesterol level during December–January of each year was 277.6, or 7.6 milligrams higher than in the June–July period.

There was no apparent reason for the winter rise in cholesterol. The variations could not be explained by weight gain or by a difference in summer and winter diets. The researchers concluded that the winter increase in cholesterol wasn't enough to cause any medical concern, but it did raise more fundamental questions about the mechanism of cholesterol in the body.

In the next chapter we're going to look at how you can begin to put this growing body of information to work to change your own personal cardiovascular risk profile. Are you one of the people who have special risks that require special attention? Who needs to be screened for high cholesterol? How reliable are the results of cholesterol screening? Which numbers are important? How often should you have your cholesterol tested? These are a few of the important questions that need to be answered before you can begin to put oat bran and other cholesterol-lowering foods to work for you.

2

Checking Your Cholesterol

Clearly, cholesterol is a major culprit in America's high incidence of coronary artery disease. High blood-cholesterol levels are in most cases a consequence of lifelong dietary excesses that begin early in childhood. These habits, set early in life, are difficult to break later on. Although heart attacks are most common in people over age fifty, the process of atherosclerosis that leads to heart disease begins much earlier.

Autopsy studies of young men killed in Korea and Vietnam showed that atherosclerosis was already well established in a large percentage. Studies from a Bogalusa, Louisiana, group have shown that fatty streaks are even present in the coronary arteries of pre-teenagers. Finnish children have the highest serum cholesterol levels in the world because of a diet high in saturated fat. And Finland has the highest mortality rate from coronary heart disease in the world. Similarly, American children increasingly are found with elevated cholesterol levels, probably due to the quantities of french fries, cookies and chocolate candy, milkshakes, hot dogs, and other junk food they eat. Cholesterol levels in childhood are the most important predictor of adult cholesterol levels and it's becoming public knowledge that we have to pay closer attention to what our children eat.

In contrast, in China the low intake of dietary fat, particularly saturated fats, has resulted in far fewer heart attacks than in the United States. China does not even rate heart disease among its ten leading causes of death. In the Mediterranean countries where olive oil, pasta, grains, and vegetables are staples, the incidence of heart disease is similarly low. The same used to be true of Japan, where the diet once centered around grains, fish, and vegetables. But as the Japanese diet has become more Westernized, the national rate of death from heart disease has shot up.

All of this information is beginning to change the way we look at diet and nutrition in America. But elevated cholesterol is an insidious problem—symptomless—and may go undetected for years while the condition worsens. How can the average American keep track of cholesterol levels?

Cholesterol-screening sites are springing up in shopping malls, at workplaces, in pharmacies, and in a variety of community and medical settings. The Centers for Disease Control report that death rates from heart disease in the United States have dropped from 286 deaths per 100,000 people in 1960 to 180 deaths per 100,000 in 1985, a one-third reduction. Much of the credit for the drop has been attributed to a 4 percent fall in cholesterol levels over the same period. Whole communities, whose leaders have become alerted to the problem, have gone on cholesterol-screening drives. In 1986 the percentage of Americans whose blood cholesterol had been checked rose to 46 percent from 35 percent three years earlier.

These statistics are promising and encouraging, but they have barely made a dent in the massive numbers of Americans thought to be at risk. Most people whose blood cholesterol is too high still aren't aware of it. According to a recent Harris poll, 79 percent of us don't even know what our cholesterol levels should be. That means that even if we've gone through a shopping mall and had our cholesterol checked (still, an unlikely occurrence in most of the United States), we don't know what the numbers mean. Even if we do know, we tend to forget it, or fail to act on the information. The problem has been compounded by our physicians who, until recently, haven't been taking the situation very seriously.

Fortunately, change is in the wind, as physicians around the country have been impressed with the validity of new research studies that show without question a direct relationship between elevated blood cholesterol and heart disease.

Wide-scale screening for cholesterol and other risk factors, and appropriate counseling for diet, is vastly cheaper and less traumatic than surgery, drugs, and extended stays in the hospital, which are typical of the high-tech intervention approach to heart disease practiced in America today.

Curbing the killer epidemic depends on two vital factors. The first is identifying the population most at risk, and the second is treating those people discovered to have elevated cholesterol. Both prongs of the attack depend on widespread education for the public and for the medical community at large.

While widespread screening is eminently desirable, it presents several problems. Not every community has a screening program, or if it does, it may conduct the program only once a year. Further, screening for cholesterol is not as easy as screening for other health problems such as high blood pressure. Screening for high blood pressure requires only the familiar blood pressure cuff and a gauge. Anyone can be taught to measure blood pressure in just a few minutes. Detailed cholesterol screening requires a blood sample and complex analysis. As a result, getting your cholesterol checked may depend largely on you.

Screening for cholesterol raises many questions about accuracy, costs, and availability.

Q: *Who needs to have their cholesterol checked?*
A: Last October the National Heart, Lung and
    Blood Institute (NHLBI) issued a report urging
    physicians to screen every adult patient over the
    age of twenty for cholesterol. Some physicians
    today recommend that even younger people have
    their blood cholesterol checked.

Adults with Elevated Cholesterol Levels*

Age	% Borderline High (200–239)	% High (240+)
20–24	20.5	6.2
25–34	18.0	16.3
35–44	33.0	28.0
45–54	35.1	36.9
55–64	37.3	36.8
65–74	32.8	24.9
All adults (20–74)	31.2	24.9

Q: *Is cholesterol screening the only way I can tell if
    I have high cholesterol?*
A: Probably. Some people with very high choles-
    terol have yellow fatty deposits in the skin called
    xanthomatosis, but most people display no out-
    ward sign if their cholesterol is elevated.

Q: *How do I get my cholesterol level checked?*
A: Your physician can order a laboratory test for
    you. Total cholesterol can also be measured by
    portable testing machines, which produce results
    in minutes at minimal cost. These on-location
    screening sites can test total serum cholesterol in

*Compiled from data from the National Heart, Lung and
Blood Institute and the National Center for Health Statistics.

three minutes just by pricking your finger. At least one person in four who are tested for total cholesterol will be told that his or her level is too high, and may be advised to see a doctor for remeasurement.

Q: *I had one cholesterol test, and now my doctor wants me to have a complete cholesterol work-up, but it costs almost $100. Is there any other way, besides the test, that I could tell if I am developing heart disease?*

A: Even a complete cholesterol breakdown cannot tell you if you are actually developing heart disease—it can only tell you if you have one of the major risk factors—but most experts believe such a test gives the best picture of what might be going on in your arteries. However, there are other indicators that can also help assess your risk, and screening for these may be as important as cholesterol screening when it comes to preventing heart disease. This kind of screening costs nothing because you can do it yourself. The more indicators, or risk factors, you have, the more likely it is that you are a candidate for heart disease, and the more urgent for you to have a cholesterol test. For example, first-degree relatives of individuals who suffered a heart attack or required open-heart surgery before the age of fifty are high risk. People with diabetes are at risk. So are those with high blood pressure. Other risk factors include being male, cigarette smoking, and severe obesity.

Q: *What is the safe level of cholesterol?*

A: Safe levels of cholesterol used to be adjusted according to age and, overall, were considerably higher than they are today. Recently, however, the National Heart, Lung and Blood Institute sharply reduced the safety zone and set a single standard of desirable blood cholesterol for everyone twenty or older.

Here's how the numbers stack up, measured in total cholesterol milligrams per deciliter of blood:

Desirable, "safe" blood cholesterol: below 200
Borderline high blood cholesterol: 200–239
High blood cholesterol: 240 and above.

There are certain variables within these guidelines: if you fall into the borderline category but show evidence of heart disease, or if you have two or more additional risk factors, you would be classified as high risk.

Q: *How do these numbers correlate with actual heart disease?*

A: The dangers of elevated cholesterol are evident: once the cholesterol level goes over 200, the chance of a heart attack doubles with every 50 mg/dl increase.

Q: *Does it matter what time of day I get tested?*

A: Test results are not affected by the actual time of day, but they may be affected by food absorption. Triglyceride levels, for example, are elevated by food and alcohol. The instant cholesterol test can be taken any time, but the more extensive laboratory test usually requires a fasting state. Therefore, detailed cholesterol tests are usually given after a 12-hour fast, which for most people means the test is carried out first thing in the morning. However, some researchers feel that more at-risk individuals would be detected if cholesterol testing was done on a full stomach.

Q: *I've heard that some people have two cholesterol tests. Is this necessary?*

A: In the interest of accuracy, the National Heart, Lung and Blood Institute recommends two tests, given one to two months apart. Your cholesterol level would be the average of the two tests. However, if the difference between the two tests is more than 30 milligrams, you should have a third test and average all three.

Q: *Just how accurate are the cholesterol tests?*

A: The accuracy of cholesterol tests has been questioned. Faulty equipment, undertrained technicians, lack of regulation chemical standards, and poor interpretation are cited as reasons for misleading test results. Even when cholesterol screening is done by a reliable laboratory (and it is not always), there is an estimated plus or minus factor of about 15 percent, either because of testing errors or variations in actual cholesterol. With a test result of 200, for example, the real reading might be as low as 170 or as high as 230. This is the reason that more than one test is recommended.

Q: *My cholesterol test was high and I was told to have another test right away. Why?*

A: Anyone found to have a high cholesterol level should undergo another test as soon as possible, especially if the original test only measured total cholesterol. The second test should include HDL cholesterol and triglycerides. The results of the second test will determine whether cholesterol-lowering treatment is advisable.

Q: *My cholesterol test is well within the normal range. How often should I be retested?*

A: You should have your cholesterol remeasured at least once every five years. However, if you have other risk factors for coronary heart disease, you should consider being tested more often.

Q: *What kind of people have the worst cholesterol ratings?*

A: The male kind. More than one-third of American men between the ages of 45 and 64 are in the high-risk category.

Q: *What does "total" cholesterol mean?*

A: Total blood cholesterol is composed of HDL and LDL.

Q: *Is the screening you get at the shopping mall as good as a test ordered by a physician?*

A: As far as discovering your total blood cholesterol, it is probably fine. The problem is that total cholesterol does not give a complete picture of your cholesterol profile. Portable analyzers cannot break down the various fats in the blood and calculate LDL and HDL levels; Even many laboratories are unable to give consistently accurate counts. Yet these figures may be the most vital statistics of all in evaluating cardiovascular health. In fact, 40 percent of patients with coronary artery disease have *normal total cholesterol levels*, a statistic reported by the Bogalusa Heart Study from Louisiana State University's Specialized Center of Research on Atherosclerosis.

Q: *Why can't the portable screening centers provide a detailed analysis?*

A: Assessing detailed cholesterol tests requires knowledge and expertise in the various lipids. Blood samples must be drawn from the vein, and a separate test is performed for triglycerides. The laboratory that analyzes the tests must specialize in coronary risk assessment, and the analysis must be carried out by a trained technician.

Q: *Is there any other way that I could tell which part of my total cholesterol is good and which is bad?*

A: No. Only sophisticated screening tests can analyze cholesterol in your blood and give it to you in fractions.

Q: *What does "ratio" of cholesterol mean?*
A: Ratio means total cholesterol divided by HDL. For example, an overall cholesterol reading of 180 and an HDL of 60 produce a ratio of 3. Most cholesterol experts today agree that your cholesterol ratio is much more important in assessing cardiac risk than total cholesterol. Some cardiologists favor the ratio of LDL to HDL, particularly in people whose LDL values are high. This ratio is calculated by dividing the LDL value by the HDL value.

Q: *What is a safe ratio?*
A: Different researchers have come up with different figures, and presently there is no standard safe ratio of total cholesterol to HDL ratio. Dr. William Castelli, medical director of the Framingham Heart Study, uses 4.5 as the top cutoff for men; above that ratio, men are considered at risk for heart disease. Other researchers place the ratio slightly lower.

For women the ratio of total cholesterol to HDL is also lower. Dr. Kenneth H. Cooper, director of the Aerobics Center in Dallas, Texas, uses a cutoff of 3.0 for women aged forty to fifty-nine. The average female heart disease victim has a ratio of 4.6 to 6.4, compared with the average male heart disease victim whose ratio is 5.4 to 6.1

Overall, the higher your ratio, the greater your risk of having a heart problem. The lower, the better.

Q: *What is the target number for LDL?*
A: It is suggested that everybody should aim for an LDL level of 130 or lower. LDL is considered the key figure in assessing risk. In cholesterol

tests the value for LDL is often calculated, rather than actually measured. That is, it is arrived at by subtracting HDL from total cholesterol.

Q: *Is it important to know your HDL level?*
A: It is becoming more important every day. The Helsinki study indicated that raising HDL levels lowered the risk of heart disease, and so many cholesterol experts today are leaning more toward the idea that low HDLs are significant. Some scientists believe that HDL is an important factor all by itself (it is estimated that 60 percent of heart attack patients have low HDLs, even though their LDLs are only moderately high); others think it is important only insofar as it relates to LDL. Either way, HDL is daily becoming more of an important cholesterol factor. While the role of HDLs is not absolutely clear, the answer would seem to be, yes, it is important to know your HDL level. Many people would go untreated if their HDL levels were not taken into account.

Q: *How high should HDL be?*
A: There is no specific target number for HDL, but most heart attacks occur in people with readings of less than 40 milligrams of HDL. Studies reported at a recent meeting of the American Heart Association in November 1988 presented evidence that, even with a total cholesterol reading in the supposedly safe zone, a person can be at risk if his HDL level is below 35. Normal HDL levels then are usually said to be 45 to 50 for men and 50 to 60 for women. The higher the HDL level, the better. Although scientists are still uncertain about the role of HDL in heart disease, HDL levels in the 70s and 80s are thought to be in some way protective.

Q: *Will raising HDL alone lower a person's risk of heart disease?*

A: There is no absolute proof that raising HDL alone can lower a person's risk of heart disease. So far clinical trials to test whether raising HDL alone will be beneficial have never been set up. In one new animal study, researchers are injecting a synthetic HDL compound into rabbits to see if raising HDL protects them against atherosclerosis. Should such experiments succeed, it is conceivable that synthetic HDL could one day become an effective treatment for heart patients. Despite the lack of hard evidence about direct beneficial effect, raising HDL could help improve cholesterol ratio, which may be a more important indicator than total cholesterol.

Q: *Is it necessary to have triglycerides measured at the same time as the cholesterol test?*

A: Some researchers, but not all, consider it helpful to measure triglycerides along with cholesterol. Whether elevated triglyceride levels by themselves increase coronary risk is still in dispute. If total cholesterol is not high, however, elevated triglycerides do not appear to be a risk factor. What the analysts are looking at when they measure triglyceride levels is its relationship to HDL. High triglyceride is linked to low HDL; low triglyceride is linked to high HDL. According to Dr. Scott M. Grundy of the University of Texas Health Science Center in Dallas, when high triglyceride levels are accompanied by low HDL, risk may be increased. In a detailed cholesterol test, triglycerides are usually included.

Q: *What is a normal triglyceride level?*

A: For men, normal triglyceride levels are 100 to 120. For women, however, somewhat lower values are recommended. For some reason, women appear to be at higher risk for heart disease if triglycerides are high. High triglycerides are usually not treated until the level reaches 200.

Q: *Why are men more likely to have heart disease than women?*

A: Men have three times more heart attacks early in life than women. The reasons given are stress, diet, smoking, and simply being male.

Q: *Are women in some way protected against high cholesterol levels?*

A: To a degree. Before menopause, women appear to have some degree of protection against high cholesterol because of the estrogen circulating in their bloodstream. Estrogen seems to encourage the liver to turn out more good HDL cholesterol. In later years, though, this advantage is lost, and women between fifty-five and sixty-four often have higher total cholesterol levels than men the same age. Correspondingly, while women have fewer early heart attacks, they gradually catch up as they grow older. Heart disease is the leading cause of death in women over age sixty-five.

New studies show that even younger women are losing some of their natural advantages. For one thing, cigarette smoking and stress are making a young woman's heart profile look more like a man's. For another, modern life is taking its toll on women's hearts. Birth control pills, choosing not to have children, surgery to remove ovaries—all appear to have some indirect effect on the heart because in one way or another they alter the hormonal balance in a woman's bloodstream. Taken together, all of these factors make it extremely important for women to look carefully at their life-style and cholesterol levels.

Q: *Do women have any other natural protectants against heart disease, besides low cholesterol?*

A: Possibly. Estrogen may help keep blood vessel linings smoother by lowering damaging stress-related hormones. New research suggests that women's coronary arteries may be more elastic, therefore more heart-disease resistant, than men's are.

Q: *Does cholesterol affect women in the same way it does men?*

A: We don't know nearly as much about the effects of cholesterol in women because most of the coronary risk trials have been carried out only in men. It may turn out that a woman has a cholesterol profile entirely different from a man's.

There appears to be some difference in the way a woman's body handles the fractions of cholesterol. For example, women tend to have higher levels of good HDL cholesterol, as well as higher levels of HDL-2, the heroic subfraction thought to work overtime to rid the arteries of plaque. In addition, animal studies have shown that after a four-week high-cholesterol diet female monkeys had much more Apo A-1—another beneficial protein that attaches itself to HDL and seeks out fat—than male monkeys.

On the down side, early research suggests that higher levels of Apo B and triglycerides may put women at greater risk of heart disease, even when their total cholesterol count is normal. Apo Bs are the proteins linked to LDLs; triglycerides are fats that the body converts to LDLs.

Q: *If older women take estrogen supplements, is it good for their hearts?*

A: Some early studies indicated that extra estrogen either increases or has no effect on heart disease risk in postmenopausal women, but that view has changed. Most researchers now believe that estrogen supplements decrease cardiac risk. There's a catch. Most estrogen therapy today is given in combination with a second hormone, progestin, to protect against endometrial cancer.

Progestin seems to reduce estrogen's heart-positive effects. For these reasons, experts urge women to have a thorough physical examination and a talk with their physician before deciding for or against hormone replacement therapy. Meanwhile, a large new study is underway on the relationship between female hormones and heart disease. Soon it should start providing more answers to the tantalizing question of estrogen's role in women's heart health.

Q: *Are women screened differently than men?*
A: No, but because of these new findings about the way cholesterol balances in women, it is especially important for a woman to have full cholesterol breakdown, including total cholesterol, LDL, HDL, the ratio of total to HDL cholesterol, and triglycerides.

Q: *Should I have my child's cholesterol checked?*
A: Evidence that heart disease begins in childhood is accumulating rapidly. New studies indicate that one-quarter to one-third of American children have high cholesterol, and most of those are in families with a history of cholesterol or heart problems. The American Academy of Pediatrics has recently urged physicians to test cholesterol levels in all children 2 years and older who have a family history of high cholesterol or premature heart attack.

Q: *What is a safe cholesterol range for my child?*
A: A cholesterol level of 140 to 150 milligrams is considered desirable in children. The danger zone is above 175.

Q: *What should I do if my child's cholesterol is elevated?*
A: The academy recommends that children whose cholesterol levels are above 175 be counseled on

their diet by nutrition specialists and taught how foods affect their health and well-being. Nutritionists also will advise parents on altering their child's diet to lower cholesterol.

Q: *Aren't children supposed to have fat in their diets?*

A: Yes, very young children do require dietary fat for normal growth. In the first two years of life, children grow very rapidly and normal development depends on sufficient calories from fat. Breast milk is 52 percent fat; formula is required to be 30 to 54 percent fat. When a baby is weaned, it should be weaned to whole milk. Only when a child is past age two should parents begin to consider moderating his or her fat intake, and even then pediatricians caution that they should not go to extremes in reducing fats in the diets of their children. The most wholehearted recommendation is to reduce junk food to an absolute minimum.

Q: *What are the dietary guidelines for children?*

A: The best guideline is moderation and consultation with your pediatrician. Children from high-risk families will need closer observation and possibly more fat restriction than other children, so family history becomes an important element in determining your child's diet. The American Heart Association recently called for the same 30 percent limit on intake of fat for children over the age of two.

Q: *My cholesterol test showed that I had normal total cholesterol, but my HDLs were low. How can I raise HDL level?*

A: Several life-style modifications can raise HDL level—regular aerobic exercise, weight loss, an end to smoking, eating a lot of fish, and drinking alcohol only in moderation.

Q: *What dietary changes should I make to reduce my triglyceride level?*

A: The relationship between diet and triglycerides is still unclear, but research continues to develop in this area. Carbohydrate intake has been associated with elevated triglycerides, but Dr. James Anderson found that triglyceride levels came down in 9 out of 10 of his hypertriglyceridemic patients who added large quantities of oat bran to their diets. Those patients who had normal triglyceride levels showed no change with oat bran consumption. For now, the best way to reduce triglycerides are to get down to your ideal body weight, engage in regular aerobic exercise, and add oat bran to your diet.

Q: *Is high cholesterol more dangerous in people who have high blood pressure?*

A: Yes. High cholesterol levels pose a particularly sinister threat for people who have high blood pressure. High blood pressure itself is a major risk factor for coronary artery disease: the greater the blood pressure, the greater the risk of coronary heart disease in both sexes at all ages. At the same time, other risk factors for coronary artery disease tend to cluster together more in people who have high blood pressure. So you could say hypertensives are overexposed to heart disease.

Uncontrolled, high blood pressure kills in three ways—stroke, kidney failure, and heart disease. Controlling blood pressure by medication can virtually eliminate stroke and kidney failure, but has had little impact on coronary heart disease. One reason for this may be that while blood pressure may come down with treatment, cholesterol levels remain unchanged. Some of the medications used to control the blood pressure may also have a negative effect on cholesterol. It is imperative that hypertensive patients have their cholesterol levels watched closely and their medications reviewed. Newer antihypertensive drugs are now available that may have either a neutral effect, or a positive lowering effect, on blood cholesterol.

Q: *I have diabetes, and my doctor says I should be especially careful about cholesterol. Why?*

A: Like hypertension, diabetes in itself is a major risk factor for heart disease. Diabetes accelerates atherosclerosis. Data from the Framingham Heart Study indicate that the presence of diabetes is associated with a two- to threefold increase in the risk of atherosclerosis. Seventy percent of premature diabetes-related deaths are caused by heart disease. Every person who has been diagnosed with diabetes should consult a dietitian and carefully follow nutritional guidelines designed to prevent heart disease.

Q: *Will reducing fat intake prevent diabetes?*

A: Reducing fat intake almost automatically reduces obesity and, therefore, should help reduce the prevalence of Type II diabetes. Even more important, however, is that reducing fat helps slow down atherosclerosis. If you are diabetic, reducing fat in your diet can save your life. Adding soluble fiber to your diet may also help; soluble fiber appears to slow the absorption of carbohydrates. Dr. Anderson found that large quantities of oat bran led to a reduced dependence on insulin and other drugs for many of his diabetic patients.

Q: *How much cholesterol is safe for the average person to eat?*

A: For several years now the American Heart Association and others have recommended that daily dietary cholesterol intake be limited to a maximum of 300 milligrams. The average egg yolk contains about 250 to 300 milligrams of cholesterol.

Q: *Is it necessary to make dietary changes if my cholesterol is normal?*

A: It's a good question, and one that scientists are gnashing their teeth over. Some experts feel most people with normal cholesterol need not make dietary changes, because dietary intake isn't always an exact predictor of blood-cholesterol levels. But many physicians and medical organizations urge low-cholesterol low-fat diets for everyone to keep total cholesterol levels within the safely low range below 200.

Q: *If my cholesterol level is borderline, do I need to do anything about it, or just watch it?*

A: Many physicians would recommend taking immediate anticholesterol action in terms of diet and exercise. Atherosclerosis is a progressive disease, meaning that it builds up over a period of years. Reducing your cholesterol even a little before too much damage is done vastly improves your risk profile for the future.

Q: *My cholesterol level was high, and my doctor recommended that I follow a cholesterol-lowering diet. I don't know whether the diet is working or not. Should I be retested?*

A: Yes. You cannot tell if your cholesterol levels are coming down unless you get tested. If you are on a cholesterol-lowering diet, or if you are taking drug treatment to lower cholesterol, your total cholesterol and HDL cholesterol should be remeasured again in at least three months or even sooner, depending on your initial reading. The higher your original cholesterol level, the more critical it is to test. If the diet is working, plan to have your cholesterol checked every three months for the first year.

Q: *I have successfully lowered my cholesterol below 200. Do I have to continue to have my choles-*

terol checked? I know that the diet I'm following has produced results.

A: According to the panel of specialists at the NHLBI, if you once had high cholesterol and have successfully brought down the level through diet, you still require routine monitoring of your blood cholesterol. You should have your cholesterol checked twice a year to make sure your blood levels are on track.

Q: *What is the recommended cholesterol-lowering diet plan?*

A: The initial anticholesterol diet limits saturated fats to 10 percent of total daily calories, and cholesterol to 300 milligrams or less. If this diet fails to lower cholesterol in three months, a second-phase, more stringent plan should be tried: 7 milligrams of saturated fat and no more than 200 milligrams of cholesterol.

Q: *Will high cholesterol levels always respond to changes in diet?*

A: No. For some people, no matter how careful they are about fats and cholesterol in their diets, no matter how much they exercise, their blood cholesterol will not come down. Usually when this happens the cholesterol problem is caused by genetics, and drug therapy is nearly always required to bring cholesterol levels down. However, the NHLBI emphasized in its report that diet is the first line of defense against high cholesterol. Drugs should be prescribed only if an intensive cholesterol-lowering diet has failed. Even if you must resort to drug therapy to lower cholesterol, it's important that you continue to follow the principles of a low-cholesterol, low-fat diet.

Doctors like to say that heart disease is "multifactorial" in origin, meaning that it stems from many contributing causes. Some of these causes are specific and incontrovertible: smoking, genetics, high blood cholesterol, hypertension. Others are controversial. It seems logical that obesity would contribute to heart disease, but will losing weight help your cholesterol level? It also seems reasonable that exercise would be good for your heart, but what kind and how much? Does exercise really have any effect on cholesterol? And what about invisible, ubiquitous stress? Can stress make cholesterol go up, and will reducing it make cholesterol go down? Do our bodies naturally compensate for the wear and tear imposed by just being alive? The answers aren't perfect, but the growing body of knowledge about these potential heart dangers is leading toward a better understanding of how our bodies normally work, and how we can keep them functioning in peak condition.

3

How Weight Loss, Exercise, and Relaxation Affect Your Cholesterol

America's growing commitment to fitness over the last two decades reflects a realization that exercise, weight maintenance, and stress relief can improve the quality of life and help lower the risk of heart disease. Diet and weight loss have been a pivotal part of this enthusiasm for fitness. Humans can and do eat anything that provides the essential materials needed to build the body and supply the fuel that drives it. In different cultures at different times in history, humans have eaten a startlingly wide array of materials. Most plants and animals have been brought to our table at one time or another. One reason that humans as a species successfully continue to thrive, while many other species dwindle into extinction, is that we can adapt ourselves to a wide range of food sources. Having such an efficient digestive and metabolic system is perhaps our greatest evolutionary asset.

Like all assets, our ability to eat almost everything has its downside. We have developed a taste for a bewildering variety of foods, and as a result some of us are attracted to the low-end of the nutritional scale, and many of us overeat. In America one person in four is overweight; studies such as the one from Framingham have shown that people who are obese have a much higher likelihood of suffering from arthritis, high blood pressure, stroke, and heart attack.

In our uniquely paradoxical fashion, we American humans are also obsessed with being slender. At any given time, some 20 million Americans are on some sort of weight-loss diet, and this obsession has led us into some dangerous eating habits—eating binges alternating with fasting. Many studies have found that 95 percent of those who lose weight will regain it within a few months.

Finding a way to control weight with the foods that also enhance our lives and extend our lifespan is an important goal. Weight control is an important factor in lowering the risk of coronary heart disease, high blood pressure, and diabetes, and it plays a significant role in any cholesterol-reducing plan. Obese individuals tend to have low HDL-cholesterol levels, the good cholesterol that helps fight heart disease. Weight loss can raise HDL cholesterol, lower the bad LDL cholesterol, and improve the cholesterol ratio.

Overweight people who begin a cholesterol-lowering diet almost always lose weight automatically because, gram for gram, vegetables, fruits, grains, and other complex carbohydrates contain fewer calories than fats. Every carbohydrate gram has 4 calories, while every gram of fat has more than twice that number. By replacing fats with complex carbohydrates, you reduce calories, even though you may actually be eating more food. Most complex carbohydrates like beans, whole grains, peas, fruits, and vegetables are also excellent sources of fiber.

Another vital component of a cholesterol-lowering, heart-protective life-style is relaxation. It is obvious that we live in a high-stress society—stress is virtually inescapable for most of us. Stress is implicated as a significant component of physical ailments ranging from heart disease and hypertension to mental breakdown and perhaps even some cancers. And yet the nature of stress is elusive. Everyone does not respond to it in the same way, and some people do not respond to it at all. There are people who genuinely thrive on conflict, and many others who fall apart under strain. (When we call stress something else—excitement, drive, competitiveness—it can have positive aspects.)

Stress can be emotional, environmental, or physical. However it is experienced, it can drastically affect our bodies. In their classic assessment of stress risks, Drs. Thomas H. Holmes and Richard H. Rake, psychiatrists at the University of Washington Medical School, interviewed nearly 400 people of various ages and backgrounds, asking each one to rank a series of life events on a scale of 1 to 100. Marriage was considered the "average" stress event and given 50 points. Participants were asked to assign higher or lower points to other life events based on their relativity to marriage. At the top of everyone's list with the highest impact of 100 points was death of a spouse. Divorce ranked second in the line of stress. At the bottom of the list, but still considered stressful, were the Christmas holiday and traffic tickets.

In a subsequent search of health statistics the researchers discovered that many widows and widowers die soon after losing their spouses. And divorced people have a twelvefold increase in illness rate after their divorce. Dr. Holmes and Dr. Minoru Masuda later verified these findings with a study of 88 patients with major illnesses. They were able to associate 93 percent of all the illness with the accumulation of stressful life changes.

The critical finding of the stress scale was that not only negative events were stress-provoking. The investigators found that all life changes, good and bad, create stress. Stress, then, came to be defined not as an event in itself, but as the product of change. Moving, getting married or divorced, losing a loved one, making decisions about conflicts, a change in your financial picture, holidays and vacations, job changes, injury or illness, children leaving home are all causes of stress.

Prolonged stress, stress that has no outlet, multiple stress events—all can place strain on our internal organs and affect our bodies in ways that are invisible until we become sick. Only in very recent years have we been able to scientifically measure some of the effects of stress on our bodies and discover antidotes to its insidious work.

A third fitness component is exercise. Energetic, regular exercise should be a part of everyone's lifestyle, particularly people concerned with weight loss or weight maintenance. Exercise helps speed up the body's metabolic rate, making it easier to keep weight under control. Anything that helps burn calories is a good adjunct to dieting. One pound of fat equals 3,500 calories and exercising uses up calories.

Dieting alone can make you lose weight, but what you really want to do is lose fat. The reason people look flabby after weight loss is that they have lost lean body tissue. Exercise maintains lean muscle tissue, while it helps you lose fat. Exercise tones up the body and makes you look better and feel stronger.

The relationship between weight, exercise, and heart disease continues to be in a state of flux. Evidence continues to accumulate that regular aerobic exercise prevents heart disease. While the benefits of strenuous aerobic exercise such as jogging and cycling are well-known, new studies reveal the benefits of more moderate exercise. It looks as if milder forms of exercise may be as heart-beneficial as more rigorous workouts. A recent Minnesota study showed that middle-aged men at high risk for heart disease were able to reduce their risk by one-third simply by engaging in moderate physical activity. The continuing study of 17,000 Harvard College alumni also suggests that moderate physical exercise can increase life expectancy. In a nutshell, even moderate exercise carried out on a fairly regular basis is good for your heart.

One great appeal of exercise, in terms of improved quality of life, is the remarkable sense of well-being it produces. Theoretically, this response is caused by the body's reaction to strong muscular activity: extra brain chemicals are released to make the exertion less painful. The longer muscular effort continues, the more chemicals are released, and the more euphoric the person feels. These unusual brain chemicals are called endorphins.

Certain forms of mental activity, including meditation and yoga techniques, can also produce endorphins. The production of endorphins can also be stimulated by mild pain—such as the prick of a needle. This may be one factor behind successful acupuncture.

In addition to its many other benefits exercise is also a good antidote to boredom, one common reason that many of us overeat. Weight maintenance and exercise are closely tied together. Stress release and exercise are also closely linked. And all three components can have considerable impact on your cholesterol level and, subsequently, your heart risk profile.

Q: *Can I lower cholesterol by losing weight?*
A: Yes. If you are overweight and have high cholesterol, losing even a few pounds will probably reduce your total cholesterol. It is relatively easy to lower total cholesterol; selectively increasing HDL is more difficult.

Q: *My girlfriend says she lost a lot of weight by adding bran to her food, but my doctor says bran is dangerous. Is she endangering her health?*
A: Whether bran is good or bad seems to depend on the type of bran and how much of it you eat.

Your physician is probably talking about wheat bran, an insoluble fiber that, when consumed in too large quantities, can strip the body of important minerals. In moderate quantities, however, wheat bran, like all other fibers, can safely help control weight. Wheat bran, by the way, belongs to a different class of fibers than oat bran, and has very different actions within the body. (See Chapter 4.)

Q: *How does fiber help you lose weight?*

A: Most people who have used fiber in the form of bran to lose weight say the greatest benefit is that it helps them stay on a low-calorie diet without ever feeling deprived. Once the full amount of fiber has been incorporated into the diet, many people cease to even notice that they are dieting. Dietary fiber in any form helps control your appetite because you don't feel hunger pangs. Because high-fiber foods are also complex carbohydrates, most people seem to lose their desire for desserts and candy. High-fiber intake lowers the level of blood insulin that stimulates your desire for food, especially sweets.

Including oats, wheat bran, and other high-fiber foods in your diet also replaces higher-calorie and high-fat foods, and thus reduces your overall caloric intake. All fibers add bulk to your system, helping you to feel full even when the calorie intake is low.

High-fiber foods make it easier to stick to a low-calorie diet because they take longer to eat and make you feel fuller for a longer period of time. Oat bran actually slows down the rate that food travels through your stomach. At the same time, oat bran and other fibers speed the rate at which food passes through the digestive tract and act as a kind of natural laxative, so there is additional caloric loss through faster intestinal elimination. Beyond all of these weight-losing benefits, and even more important from a health standpoint, including high-fiber foods in your diet can help make long-term weight control a permanent part of your life.

Q: *How exactly is stress defined?*

A: Stress is the nonspecific bodily response to any physical or emotional demand. Stress is produced by major life crises as well as everyday events. Stress is neither positive nor negative; it is experienced by everyone, but handled in different ways.

The nature of the stress event itself is less important than a person's ability to cope with it. When ordinary daily stress is managed well, it contributes to enhanced thinking and creativity, high energy level, endurance, and improved physical performance.

Q: *My job creates a lot of stress in my life. Could it be making my cholesterol levels high?*

A: It might. In one well-known study, cholesterol levels of accountants rose significantly during stressful weeks preceding April 15, and dropped back down to normal after the income tax due date passed. Dr. Meyer Friedman, co-author with Dr. Ray Rosenman of *Type A Behavior and Your Heart,* first theorized that high-strung, anxious, "stressed out" people were more vulnerable to heart disease and elevated cholesterol levels than more relaxed individuals.

Q: *Can relaxation techniques lower cholesterol?*

A: Recently, despite the continuing skepticism of some cardiologists, relaxation techniques such as yoga and meditation have taken their place in the conventional medical armamentarium. Dramatic evidence that relaxation works was shown by Dr. Dean Ornish's study in which he observed a reversal of heart disease in people with hypertension and clogged arteries. The daily regimen followed by his patients included yoga and meditation, along with a low-fat, vegetarian diet and exercise. Many of Dr. Ornish's patients were taking medication for hypertension, and most of them were able to reduce their dosage or, in many cases, stop it altogether.

Q: *My mother says I have a terrible temper and that one of these days it will give me a heart attack. Is there any evidence that losing your temper could make you drop dead?*

A: Although new research indicates that chronic anger may be hazardous to your health, it's unlikely that an occasional outburst of temper would have such dire consequences. Anger, like stress, is believed to trigger the release of catecholamines, chemicals that cause the heart to beat faster and pump harder, raising both blood pressure and cholesterol. Blowing off steam occasionally is probably harmless, but chronic, nagging anger that stays with you may be dangerous. Doing a slow burn extends the time the heart has to function at a vessel-damaging pace. If you lose your temper all the time or find yourself clenching your teeth in gut-wrenching silence, consider more positive ways to deal with anger. Some suggestions are: a daily walk or an afternoon nap, daily relaxation exercises, regular workouts and balanced, well-timed meals—all these activities seem to help keep moods on a more even keel.

Q: *How does stress cause disease?*

A: In addition to the obvious emotional disturbances provoked by stress, stress has been linked to several disease states, including heart disease, high blood pressure, strokes, ulcers, palpitations, and allergies. How stress does this insidious work is complex.

Heart rate and blood pressure are a function of the autonomic nervous system, meaning that they operate automatically and supposedly are out of our conscious control. The autonomic nervous system is a protective mechanism, that, among other duties, governs what is commonly called the "fight or flight" response.

Sudden fear or danger activates an overwhelming physical response within the body; the heart pumps faster, breathing is more rapid, blood rushes to the muscles, metabolism revs up, and blood pressure soars. "Fight or flight" describes the body's heroic response to stress. When danger threatens, we are primed instantly to fight our way out or, failing that, run to safety.

Once the danger has passed, all bodily systems return to normal. Since the earliest ages of humankind this natural life-saving reaction was part of the survival of the fittest. Fight or flight has evolved intact through millions of years probably because it was so necessary to human survival. Today, our everyday environment— loaded with pressure, stress, anxiety, competition—can still trigger this fight or flight response. Modern-day threats are more likely to be made to our emotions, not to our physical bodies. But our bodies react in the same old way—with one important difference: there is no physical release. As a result, our bodily organs suffer from internalized stress reactions.

Q: *Can just one major stress event cause a heart attack?*

A: Heart disease usually develops over a period of years, and it's unlikely that someone with healthy coronary arteries and a healthy heart muscle would have a heart attack due to a single stress event. Stress tends to be dangerous when it is cumulative. When someone is constantly faced with unrelenting stress over which they have little control, they simply may not have the biological resources to cope with it. If enough stressful changes are clustered together at one time, they leave people especially vulnerable to illness.

Having control seems to be a key element in how well people cope with stress. The more control you have over your own life events, the less effect stress has on you. In that way, the CEO of a major corporation may have less stress than the person who works on the assembly line.

Q: *What's the best way to reduce stress?*
A: One of the problems with stress is that its effects are usually invisible—you can't see it, and you can't see what it's doing to your body until you become sick. A way to reduce invisible stress was first observed in two landmark studies that measured the body's response to specific relaxation techniques.

In 1968 Dr. John I. Lacey of the Fels Research Institute in Yellow Springs, Ohio, discovered that concentration had a direct effect on heart rate and blood pressure—and vice versa. Dr. Lacey observed substantial drops in heart rate when his subjects did exacting problems in mental arithmetic. He also noticed that an excess in heart rate and blood pressure prevented a person from concentrating.

Dr. Herbert Benson, in his landmark work, *The Relaxation Response*, proved that meditation could help those people who already had high blood pressure because it produced a physiologic response directly opposite of "fight or flight." Meditating and other relaxation responses may prove to have even greater benefits for healthy people, because they have been shown to decrease blood lactate, a substance strongly linked to anxiety. During the first ten minutes of meditation, blood lactate levels drop rapidly and remain extremely low throughout meditation. This effect may block the stress mechanism that some researchers believe to cause many different ailments.

Relaxation also has been shown to help some people with adult-onset diabetes to regulate glucose. Relaxation may help those with chronic, nonseasonal asthma of the upper airways to open constricted air passages. And relaxation may lower cholesterol levels in people whose blood cholesterol is elevated.

Q: *How much stress does it take to create problems?*

A: It depends on the individual. Some people naturally have a remarkable capacity to cope with stress, and others don't. Everyone can learn to handle stress better and reduce its damaging effects.

Q: *What are the best stress relievers?*

A: There are several ways to relieve stress, but they are all part of a basic method: try to reduce the number of stressful incidents in your life; reduce the intensity of those episodes; and, finally, learn to relax during the breathing spaces in between. Relaxation can mean many things—yoga, meditation, other relaxation methods. It can mean taking a long walk or counting backwards from 100.

Regular exercise workouts provide great release from stress. The endorphins released into the bloodstream during strenuous exercise create an almost palpable sense of well-being.

The trick to stress relief is to find a relaxation technique that's right for you and fits into your life-style. There are many ways to relax and alleviate stress. Here are some ideas recommended by many experts in the stress-management field:

- Exercise to release tension
- Participate in a hobby or activity that gives you a sense of accomplishment
- Follow regular hours when it comes to meals, sleep, and exercise
- If you feel troubled, talk things over with a friend
- Try any form of meditation for 10 minutes each day
- Also try some form of physical relaxation technique—yoga, stretching, deep breathing, all help relieve stress
- Analyze the way you presently deal with stress. Much of the stress we feel is a result of our own attitude. Try changing some of the ways you react to situations that leave you feeling tense.
- It may help you to keep track of stress events in a daily log. Most people who are "stressed out" are conditioned to react to stress trigger points. That is, every time a particular situation arises they will respond in the same way out of pure habit. With some thought and attention, most people can identify their own stress trigger points.

Q: *How does exercise affect heart disease?*
A: Lack of exercise may be as heart-risky as smoking a pack of cigarettes a day or having high blood pressure or elevated cholesterol. A recent report published by the Centers for Disease Control emphasized that because it's so widespread lack of exercise could be the biggest heart danger of all: the Centers' statistics indicate that 59 percent of Americans get less than 20 minutes of physical activity three times a week.

Q: *I know I feel better when I exercise, but besides improving circulation how does exercise affect my heart?*

A: Exercise helps the heart in many different ways: exercise helps reduce moderately high blood pressure; it helps prevent blood clots; and it lowers heart rate, a marker of heart efficiency. Some experts believe that regular exercise may widen existing coronary arteries. It's been shown that regular exercise stimulates the growth of collateral vessels to the heart. If the coronary arteries are blocked, exercise will encourage these new vessels to form a kind of natural bypass around the blockage, providing additional blood flow. A good system of collateral vessels can sometimes prevent a heart attack and can lessen the likelihood of death should a heart attack occur. On top of all these benefits, people who exercise regularly are much less likely to be overweight.

Exercise also has positive benefits for those with high blood pressure, which is a major risk factor for heart disease. An interesting side effect of exercise is that those who get actively engaged in such activities as swimming and jogging tend to quit smoking cigarettes, another devastating risk factor.

Q: *Can exercise reduce high cholesterol levels?*

A: It is not clear whether exercise directly reduces high blood cholesterol, but exercise might have an indirect effect because it alleviates stress, which, in turn, can reduce cholesterol. Exercise also contributes significantly to weight loss. Weight loss in overweight individuals usually lowers high levels of blood cholesterol.

Exercise is clearly beneficial, but it cannot negate the damage done by a cholesterol-raising diet. You cannot get away with a steady diet of burgers, french fries, and shakes and hope to exercise off the fat and cholesterol.

Q: *What is the controversy about exercise and cholesterol?*

A: It isn't so much controversy as it is incomplete information. Until very recently studies seemed to show that vigorous exercise could drive up the beneficial HDL count. New studies, specifically a new work from Dr. Peter Wood and his colleagues at Stanford University, suggest that HDL may be raised, not by exercise, but by the weight loss that is a result of the exercise. Dr. Wood's study, which focused on HDL, is one of the few to distinguish between the effects of weight loss and the effects of exercise in altering cholesterol levels. His findings have important implications for people at their normal weight. Previously, it was thought that exercise could raise low HDL cholesterol in everyone. Now it seems that thin people may not be able to raise the good cholesterol by exercising. However, exercise can help those of us who are overweight lose weight, and thereby improve our cholesterol profiles.

In another study, 10 healthy men with normal cholesterol levels did 25 minutes of aerobic exercise four times a week for eight weeks. They also followed a low cholesterol diet. When the amount of cholesterol in their diets was increased to 600 milligrams, their blood cholesterol increased significantly. When their dietary cholesterol was again reduced to 200 milligrams a day, their blood cholesterol returned to normal.

Cardiologist Paul Thompson of Brown University placed 8 sedentary men on a regimen of rigorous exercise, along with closely controlled diets that maintained their weight. After 48 weeks, Dr. Thompson reported HDL had gone up an average of only 5 mg/dl. Surprisingly, the participants experienced a remarkable 16 percent drop in their triglycerides.

Q: *What kind of exercise is best for the heart?*

A: The best exercises for helping the heart are swimming, walking, bicycling and running. These aerobic-type exercises appear to lower blood pressure and reduce the pulse rate. Swimming is the least stressful of this group of exercises. Walking also places minimal strain on the heels, ankles, shins, and knee joints, and so the walker seldom suffers the pain or ligament damage often experienced by runners and joggers.

Q: *Can stopping smoking reduce my cholesterol level?*

A: Whether cigarette smoking affects cholesterol levels directly is still unknown. But smoking unquestionably is a major risk factor for heart disease, as well as emphysema and cancer. Stopping smoking can have one of the quickest positive effects on your heart.

Q: *How much exercise do I need to do?*

A: How much exercise is necessary and just how important it might be remains controversial. No one knows the optimum level, but studies indicate that even small amounts of exercise, such as climbing stairs several times a day, can be beneficial for the heart.

Moderate activity—a brisk 20-minute walk three times a week—improves your edge. A study by Dr. Arthur S. Leon found that 15 to 45 minutes of moderate daily activity such as dancing, gardening, swimming, and home exercise was beneficial.

Many studies have shown that the benefits of exercise seem to peak out, and a point of rigorousness exists beyond which there is little, if any, increased benefit to the heart. Some researchers place that point at the moderate level, and others increase it to the equivalent of running 15 miles a week. For heart protection, most experts recommend a steady aerobic workout—jogging, brisk walking, cycling, swimming—for about 30 minutes three to five times a week.

Q: *Do I need to see a doctor before I start exercising?*

A: If you are over the age of 35 or if you have any family history of heart disease, you should consult your physician before starting off on an exercise program. Also, if you are in very poor condition, if you are a heavy smoker, seriously overweight, or under treatment for a medical condition, check with your doctor before embarking on an exercise regime. You may first need to undertake supervised exercise with a trainer to work yourself into better condition. If you haven't done any physical exercise in a while, be certain to start off slowly and gradually increase your tolerance.

Q: *I know walking is good for me, but does walking provide enough exercise to benefit the heart?*

A: It's true that walking is good for everyone. Walking makes the whole body function more efficiently, and there is no doubt that walking can reduce stress and improve general well-being. Walking is almost the perfect exercise, chiefly because it fits in with most people's lifestyle and can easily be carried out in a consistent manner. In terms of heart benefits, the regularity of exercise is more important than the type of physical activity you choose. You're better off taking a brisk walk every day than playing a hard game of tennis once a week.

Q: *I think I walk a lot, but it doesn't seem to make any difference in my weight. What exercise will help me lose weight?*

A: Almost any regular exercise will help you lose weight if it is accompanied by an appropriate diet. Although walking does not take off weight rapidly, over time it can make a lot of difference. The trick is to be consistent, and keep your feet moving at a fairly brisk pace. You can burn up more than 300 calories an hour by taking a brisk walk—the faster you walk, the more your calories burn. Studies have shown that one-half hour of walking daily can result in a 15-pound weight loss over a one-year period—as long as you don't increase your caloric intake.

Q: *I have been reasonably thin all of my life, but now that I've passed the age fifty marker, I'm starting to put on weight. I don't think I'm eating any more than usual. Would exercise help?*

A: It should help. As you grow older, your metabolism slows down. The same kind and quantity of food that you ate at twenty will put weight on you at forty. To make it worse, most of us eat more and exercise even less as we grow older. The more active you are, the more calories your body burns.

Q: *I lead a very hectic life and find it virtually impossible to set aside time for a daily or even a weekly exercise routine. Is erratic exercise better than none?*

A: Yes. Any physical activity is better than being completely sedentary. Getting a regular routine going is hard for many people. Everyone is different. We all have different capacities, different demands on our time, and different things that we enjoy doing in our spare time. Some of us have easy access to gym equipment or swimming pools. Some of us enjoy sports and have the opportunity to play frequently. And some of us have none of these things. And yet with a little imagination it should be possible for everyone to engage in some kind of physical activity.

Try to make it as regular as you can. The one thing to avoid is extreme physical exercise on an occasional basis.

Each of us should choose a form of activity that we enjoy doing and that is readily accessible to us. Dancing is good exercise, and so is table tennis. So is mopping the floor and washing the windows. Here are some recommendations from physical trainers of simple ways to incorporate more physical activity into daily life:

- Look for ways to make your normal day more active. If you work at a sedentary job, make a point of getting up and walking somewhere in the office building every hour for a couple of minutes if you can. Climb up and down a flight of stairs a few times during the day. Use labor-intensive equipment rather than labor-saving devices. When you're doing errands around town, walk don't ride. Instead of catching the bus at the nearest stop, choose one a couple of stops farther on. This sort of activity will become second nature, and you will add a considerable amount of regular exercise to your week.

- Try to create a regular exercise pattern two or three times a week. Swim or work out on regular days, or try an exercise class at lunch hour or after work. If gyms and sports are not for you, and getting to a swimming pool is difficult, work out an exercise regime at home. Invest in a stationary exercise bike. Exercycles can be used in all weathers, all year round. Set it up within sight of the television set, so you can watch while you work, or listen to the radio.

- If you find the same old routine boring, mix up the kind of sports and exercise you do. All activity is good; you don't have to do the same thing day after day.

- Try to set aside a special time for exercise, and keep a daily record. Exercise with someone, if possible; make it a social event and keep track of your progress. Whatever form of exercise you choose, don't just plunge in suddenly— prepare yourself. A few aches and pains are to be expected when you first start out, but don't push yourself to muscle strain or injury.

- If possible, choose an exercise that uses your whole body, and that promotes deep breathing, sweating, and increased heartbeat: walking, running, cycling, and swimming are whole-body exercises. Weightlifting and bodybuilding, which enlarge specific muscles, are not. If you enjoy bodybuilding exercises, make sure to add some aerobic exercise, too.

- Don't attempt to get into top condition too fast. Work up gradually until you reach the time and distance limit at which you feel most comfortable. Similarly, if you use an exercise bike, gradually increase the tension against which you cycle and gradually lengthen the period you spend on it. Never push yourself beyond what feels reasonable. Exercise is never better if it hurts. After an exercise session you should feel invigorated, not devastated.

- If you enjoy competitive, highly energetic sports, make sure you first get into good condition. Struggling to win when you are in poor condition means strained muscles and possible damage to the heart.

- Don't ever go from a resting state to hard exercise. Warm-up exercises are essential to get muscles working. Similarly, after exercise, cool down exercises will keep muscles relaxed and warm until they are fully rested.

- If you feel sick or dizzy, feel a tightness in your chest, get a severe headache, or see spots while you're working out, stop exercising at once and check with your doctor as soon as possible. You may have an underlying problem that needs attention.

- For an enhanced benefit, follow exercise with a session of physical relaxation.

4

Oat Bran Makes the Difference

The Wall Street Journal reports that in 1988 sales for oat bran doubled, while oatmeal cereal sales jumped 15 percent. Why the sudden surge in oat consumption? Oat bran has been proven to effectively lower cholesterol.

The transformation of ordinary oats into a miracle food is largely the work of Dr. James W. Anderson, professor of medicine at the University of Kentucky College of Medicine. In 1976 Dr. Anderson, a specialist in diabetes, was observing the progress of a group of diabetic patients who were on a high-fiber, low-fat diet. Their blood cholesterol levels had fallen far more than could be explained by fat deprivation, and Anderson suspected that the high-fiber content of their diets was responsible. His own cholesterol level, at 285, was a cause for concern. Dr. Anderson knew of earlier European studies showing that oatmeal lowered blood cholesterol when consumed in very large quantities. He theorized that concentrated oat bran might be a more efficient method to lower cholesterol.

With some help from the Quaker Oats Company, Dr. Anderson obtained a 100-pound sack of oat bran from an oat-milling plant and began to test it in his own diet. Although his high cholesterol level could be traced to genetic inheritance, which does not always respond well to dietary treatment, Dr. Anderson proceeded to reduce his fat intake and consume substantial quantities of oat bran in the form of hot cereal and muffins. His cholesterol level plummeted 110 points, or 38 percent, in only five weeks.

Dr. Anderson's remarkable success using himself as a guinea pig led to further studies that support his initial findings. In his first experiment 4 patients consumed 100 grams of oat bran a day and achieved a 38 percent reduction in blood cholesterol. Another eight patients on the same regime achieved a 13 percent reduction in their blood cholesterol in just two weeks. Dr. Anderson and his colleagues at the University of Kentucky concluded that the use of 50 to 100 grams of oat bran daily could lower blood cholesterol an average of 19 percent, which translated into a reduction of risk of 38 percent.

In the initial studies, oat bran was added to a typical diet such as most Americans eat—a diet in which ordinary fats and cholesterol account for 37 percent of the caloric intake. When the overall diet was changed to low-fat and low-cholesterol, the results of adding oat bran were even more remarkable. Dr. Anderson found that when participants with high blood cholesterol added 50 grams of oat bran a day to a low-fat, low-cholesterol diet, their cholesterol dropped by 25 percent over a two-year period.

The best part of Dr. Anderson's findings was that oat bran lowered LDLs, while the good HDL remained untouched or actually increased. This selectivity of oat products makes them especially protective against coronary heart disease. He projects that if his subjects maintain their new blood-cholesterol levels it will reduce their risk for developing heart disease by more than 50 percent.

In 1986 Linda Van Horn, assistant professor of community and preventive medicine at Northwestern University Medical School, conducted further oat bran studies and reported that 69 people who consumed 39 grams of oat bran a day for 42 days reduced their total cholesterol by 3 percent.

Oat bran also captured the spotlight in several articles which concluded that, compared with drugs, oat bran was the least expensive method for reducing cholesterol. By the time the information had made its way into the press, oat bran was being talked about by health-conscious consumers and medical insiders. With the publication of Robert E. Kowalski's *Eight-Week Cholesterol Cure*, oat bran became famous, and the general public became aware, virtually overnight, of its remarkable properties.

The suggestion that the consumption of oats could reduce the risk of heart attack gave weight to the most significant health issue of our time, the link between diet and disease.

Fame always brings complications and controversy. Bonnie Liebman, director of nutrition for the Center for Science in the Public Interest, has been widely quoted as cautioning, "It takes a lot of oat bran to lower your cholesterol level substantially. In studies where people ate either a bowl of oatmeal or two oat bran muffins a day that contained 39 grams of oat bran, cholesterol levels dropped 2.7 percent." These figures have since been adjusted to 35 grams of oat bran equal a 3 percent drop in blood cholesterol, but it still remains a minimal reduction.

How do the realities of oat bran compare with the promises? Looking down the line from where we are right now, if you want to lower your cholesterol or maintain it at a heart-healthy level, adding oats to your diet is a simple, safe, and economical way to do it.

Q: *How does oat bran work to lower cholesterol?*
A: According to Dr. Anderson, oat bran works to lower blood cholesterol in three ways. The soluble fiber in oat bran acts like a sponge. It doubles the amount of bile acids, the fat emulsifiers

that contain cholesterol, eliminated in the feces. Oat bran also slows down the manufacture of cholesterol in the liver, giving the liver less cholesterol to release into the bloodstream. Third, by a mechanism not yet understood, oat bran selectively reduces LDL cholesterol while it raises or leaves untouched protective HDL cholesterol.

Dr. Anderson also found that large quantities of oat bran helped his diabetic patients control their blood sugar. In addition, its cholesterol-lowering effect helped reduce their risk of heart attack.

Oat bran can help control weight and protect against hypoglycemia. The soluble fiber in oat bran slows down food absorption and absorbs water in the stomach and small intestine, which gives a feeling of fullness.

Preliminary studies from Dr. Anderson also suggest that increasing fiber intake lowers blood pressure in mildly hypertensive individuals. Fifty grams of oat bran—half the amount suggested for lowering cholesterol—will result in a small reduction in blood pressure.

Q: *What's the difference between whole oats and oat groats?*

A: There is no difference, but the package labels can be confusing. A whole oat may be called a berry, a kernel, or a groat.

Working from the inside out, a whole oat grain includes the "germ" tucked into the bottom half of the grain; the large endosperm, which fills up the oat; and a layer of bran, which coats the outside. A whole oat is encased in a hull, which must be removed before the oat can be used for food. The hull is like the husk on an ear of corn.

Q: *How do you get just the oat bran?*

A: After the hull is removed, the entire oat is milled; the larger particles, the bran, are sifted from the smaller ones, which end up as flour. The oat flour is then used for commercial baked goods and animal feed.

Q: *Besides helping to lower cholesterol, does oat bran contain any nutrients?*

A: Yes. Unlike wheat bran, which is insoluble fiber that passes through your system virtually intact, oat bran supplies many important vitamins and minerals to your body. All of the nutrients found naturally in whole oats are concentrated in the bran: potassium, protein, phosphorus, iron, calcium are all present in oat bran.

The nutrient content for ⅔ cup of oat bran is approximately:

Calories	200
Protein	12 grams
Carbohydrate	32 grams
Fat	4 grams
Cholesterol	0
Sodium	0 (when prepared without salt)
Potassium	300.00 mg
Phosphorous	424.50 mg
Magnesium	143.50 mg
Calcium	46.50 mg
Iron	4.30 mg
Niacin	0.58 mg
Thiamine	0.80 mg
Riboflavin	0.13 mg
Vitamin A	0
Vitamin C	0

Q: *What are rolled oats?*

A: Rolled oats are whole oats that are steamed, then flattened by rolling. This is the most common American oatmeal. Rolled oats can be used as breakfast cereal and in many different kinds of recipes. Cooking for cereal: about 5 minutes.

Q: *How does oat bran compare to whole rolled oats?*

A: Oat bran is believed to have about twice the potency of rolled oats. It has slightly more protein and slightly less carbohydrate than rolled oats. Like whole oats, oat bran can be used as a hot cereal or incorporated into a wide variety of recipes. Cooking time for oat bran: 1–2 minutes.

Q: *What are "quick" rolled oats?*

A: Quick rolled oats are rolled oats that have been cut into pieces and heat-treated so they will cook faster. They can be used in any recipe that calls for "rolled oats." Cooking time: 1 minute.

Q: *Are "quick" rolled oats the same thing as "instant" oats?*

A: No. Instant oats are made from refined pieces of whole oats and rolled thinner than rolled oats. They often have sugar, salt, and artificial flavorings added.

Q: *What are steel-cut oats?*

A: Steel-cut oats, or Scottish or Irish oats, are whole oats that have been cut into small bits with sharp blades. They are usually made into cooked cereal called Scotch or Irish oatmeal. Steel-cut oats can be used in most recipes calling for oat flakes or oatmeal and blend well with other flours for bread baking. Cooking time: 30 minutes.

Q: *What is the difference between oat bran and wheat bran?*

A: Oat bran is soluble fiber, which is more palatable than insoluble fiber. Wheat bran, which is found in the vast majority of bran cereals, is insoluble fiber, meaning that it passes through the digestive system intact. Both kinds of fiber play important roles in good nutrition.

Both kinds of bran contain dietary fiber, the portion of plant foods that humans cannot digest. Fiber fights heart disease, high blood pressure, diabetes, and obesity. Lack of fiber has been linked to certain types of cancer, specifically colon cancer, although more research is required to establish this relationship. The more highly processed a food is, the less fiber it contains.

Q: *Which foods contain insoluble fiber?*

A: Both insoluble and soluble fibers are found in the same foods, but the amount varies. Insoluble fiber is found in large amounts in wheat bran, corn bran, and rice bran, whole grains, dried beans and peas, popcorn, seeds, and nuts; most fruit and vegetables, especially those eaten with the skin, also contain large amounts of insoluble fiber. Insoluble fiber passes through the digestive system more quickly than soluble fiber, and is well known as a natural laxative.

Q: *Does wheat bran lower cholesterol?*

A: It does not appear to lower cholesterol, but it has many other important health benefits. Insoluble fiber prevents constipation. Some medical researchers believe it lessens the risk of colon cancer by reducing the amount of time carcinogens remain in the system. Insoluble fiber may also be effective in preventing or treating diverticulosis, irritable bowel syndrome, and hemorrhoids. But too much insoluble fiber can rob the body of minerals, particularly calcium. However, this is not a danger to most Americans, who consume very little insoluble fiber in their diets.

Q: *Do other foods besides oat bran contain soluble fibers?*

A: Many foods are high in soluble fiber. Soluble

fiber is also found in barley, chick peas, black-
eyed peas, all variety of dried beans, lentils, sesame seeds, all varieties of fruits and vegetables,
especially citrus fruits, apples, pears, sweet potatoes, carrots, okra, cauliflower, and corn.

Q: *Does that mean that oat bran is not the only food
that could lower cholesterol?*

A: That's right. Any food that contains soluble fiber
can help lower cholesterol in the same way that
oat bran does. Beans are almost as good as oat
bran when it comes to lowering cholesterol, and
should be incorporated into any cholesterol-lowering plan. Barley, lentils, dried peas, and apples
are all good sources of soluble fiber.

Q: *How can I tell if oat bran is working to lower my
blood cholesterol?*

A: You can't. Everyone does not get the same result. There are no hard and fast rules or guaran-
tees when it comes to lowering blood cholesterol
by eating oats. Based on the current studies, researchers can conclude only that they seem to
work, but making sweeping predictions for the
entire population is difficult, since everybody
reacts differently.

For more effective cholesterol reduction the

The only way you can tell if oat bran is working for you is to have your cholesterol level
checked before you begin eating oat bran and
then periodically about every three months thereafter.

Q: *How much oat bran will do the job?*

A: Two new studies from Northwestern University,
sponsored by the Quaker Oats Company, indicated that 35 grams of oat bran consumed daily
caused an average 3 percent reduction in cholesterol. This is considered a slight reduction.

For more effective cholesterol reduction the

goal is ⅔ to 1 cup each day. The maximum recommended is one cup of oat bran.

What you're looking for is between 3 and 6 grams of soluble fiber, which can be found in 50 to 100 grams of oat bran. With this amount, studies have shown that blood cholesterol may be lowered by between 10 and 20 percent.

Q: *I find the measurements confusing—labels on oat bran products sometimes list grams or ounces. Recipes often call for ounces or cups. Is there an easy way to figure out how much oat bran you're getting?*

A: Most recommendations for oat bran are provided in terms of oat bran grams, but it's hard to get a picture of how much a gram is. One ounce of pure hot oat bran cereal—⅓ cup dry; ⅔ cup cooked—weighs 28 grams.

Most of us are going to measure dry oat bran in cups or ounces. Here's how it works out:

$$\begin{array}{lll} ⅓ \text{ cup} = 1 \text{ ounce} & = 28.4 \text{ grams} \\ ⅔ \text{ cup} = 2 \text{ ounces} & = 56.8 \text{ grams} \\ 1 \text{ cup} = 3 \text{ ounces} & = 85.2 \text{ grams} \end{array}$$

Q: *What are the best ways to get oat bran in your food?*

A: Most experts believe the most efficient ways to get oat bran into the diet are as a hot oat bran cereal or in homemade muffins.

Q: *Is oatmeal just as good as oat bran?*

A: Some new studies suggest that it is. Dr. James Anderson, and Dr. Kurt Gold, of the University of California at Irvine, had thought that you would have to eat about twice as much oatmeal as oat bran to get the same cholesterol-lowering effects. But the new studies from Northwestern University, under the direction of Jeremiah Stamler, indicate that hot oatmeal, which contains 20 percent less soluble fiber than oat bran, has virtually the same cholesterol-lowering effect.

Q: *Is hot oatmeal more effective in lowering blood cholesterol than cold cereal?*

A: Although many cold cereals containing oat bran may be effective in lowering cholesterol, they do not equal oat bran or hot oatmeal in their cholesterol-lowering effect. Hot oatmeal seems to get its increased potency from the actual heating process, but scientists have not yet discovered why this happens.

Q: *Every time I go to the supermarket I see a new bread or cereal with oat bran in it. How can I tell if these products are good sources of oat bran?*

A: You can't always tell. A bread or cookie, for example, which is boldly labeled "OAT" or "OATMEAL" may contain only trivial amounts of oats. Product labels often do not list the amount of specific ingredients they contain. But all products must at least list their ingredients in descending order. If oat bran, oat flour, or whole oats is not high on the ingredients list, the product probably does not contain very much in the way of oats.

The best advice is to read the label carefully; if it seems confusing or inadequate, do not rely on that product to provide you with the soluble fiber you need. (See Chapter 6.)

Q: *I have heard that products containing oat bran may also contain ingredients that raise cholesterol. Is this true?*

A: Unfortunately it is true that some products that promote themselves as high in oat bran also contain damaging saturated fats. Products such as crackers, cookies, and health bars that contain tropical oils—coconut oil or palm oil—should be avoided.

Q: *What if the cookies and crackers don't contain saturated fats—then would they be good sources of fiber?*

A: Snack foods probably don't contain much oat bran, but as long as they are healthful, they are good alternatives to foods of similar variety that don't have any oat bran at all.

Q: *What's so great about oat bran muffins? Are they any different from any other kind of oat bran product?*

A: Muffins provide large quantities of oat bran for their size and calories—one muffin contains 25 grams of oat bran, which is 25 percent of the maximum daily oat bran requirement.

Q: *If you don't make it yourself, how can you judge an oat bran muffin?*

A: Some commercial muffins contain so little oat bran that they are virtually useless as a source of fiber. Some contain such large quantities of fat and calories that, no matter how much oat bran they contain, they are not good in terms of nutrition.

In October 1988 *The New York Times* published the results of a nutritional survey of 50 oat bran muffins from 30 bakers around the country. One of the muffins evaluated contained 29 grams of fat, another had 824 calories, half of the total daily calories recommended for most women.

The best muffin was made by David's Cookies, which distributes its products in 26 states. David's 4½ ounce muffin contained 78 calories, 1 gram of fat, no cholesterol, and 16 grams of oat bran. This is almost as good as homemade. If you aren't certain that a commer-

cial oat bran muffin measures up to the one
made by David's Cookies, consider learning to
make your own. It's easy to do and is worth the
little bit of time it takes. (See Chapter 8.)

Q: *Is it really necessary to eat oat bran every day?
What difference would it make if you ate a large
quantity every other day?*

A: According to current research, whatever form of
oat bran you choose, you must eat it every day if
you expect it to lower cholesterol. Oat bran
needs to be in your system every day, just as
cholesterol is, to get the maximum cholesterol-
lowering effect.

Q: *Besides pure oat bran, which is the best oat cereal?*

A: According to a guide published by the Center for
Science in the Public Interest, after Quaker Oat
Bran Cereal, the products with the most oat bran
and the fewest calories are: Quaker Oatmeal,
Health Valley Oat Bran Hot Cereal, Kölan Oat
Bran Crunch, Health Valley Oat Bran O's,
Health Valley Oat Bran Flakes, and Kellogg
Common Sense Oat Bran. However, new products are being introduced almost daily, it seems,
and some of the most recent arrivals on your
supermarket shelves may not appear on this
chart. Careful label reading (see Chapter 6) will
help you find the most effective oat bran products.

Q: *If I eat oat bran every day, can I also eat high-
cholesterol foods like bacon and eggs?*

A: Dr. Anderson believes that oat bran works even
when people eat the "typical American diet,"
meaning the heart-damaging diet that derives 37
percent of its calories from fat. However, even if
oat bran does help, there is only so much it can
accomplish.

Oat Bran Cholesterol-Lowering Guide‡

In this chart, the highlighted column tells you about how many cookies or muffins or bowls of cereal you'd have to eat every day to lower your cholesterol by around 3 percent. If you've got to eat 10 servings, for example, multiply the calories per serving by 10 to find the true calorie cost of your oats.

Product	Serving[1]	Oat Bran (g)	Calories	Servings to Get 3% Drop
✔Quaker Oat Bran Cereal	⅓ cup, dry	28.0	90	1
✔Quaker Oatmeal, all flavors	⅓ cup, dry[2]	9.0	100	1
✔Health Valley Oat Bran Hot Cereal	¼ cup	20.0	100	2*
✔Kölln Oat Bran Crunch	⅓ cup	20.0	120	2
Health Valley Oat Bran Fruit Muffins	1 (2 oz.)	16.9-17.2	140-170	2*
✔Health Valley Oat Bran O's	¾ cup	15.0	90	2
✔Health Valley Oat Bran Flakes	½ cup	15.0	100	2*
✔Kellogg Common Sense Oat Bran	⅔ cup	13.0	100	3
Health Valley Jumbo Fruit Bars	1 (1.5 oz.)	12.5	150	3*
Kölln Fruit 'N Oat Bran Crunch Cereal	⅓ cup	11.1	110	3
Kellogg Cracklin' Oat Bran	½ cup	9.0	110	4
New Morning Oatios with Oat Bran	1 cup	8.4	110	4*
Kölln Crispy Oats Cereal	⅓ cup	8.3	110	4
General Mills Cheerios	1¼ cup	8.0	110	4
Quaker Oat Squares	½ cup	5.0	100	7
Health Valley Fruit Jumbos Oat Bran Cookies	2 (1.1 oz.)	4.6	140	8*
Health Valley Fruit & Nut Oat Bran Cookies	2 (0.8 oz.)	4.0	88	9*
New Morning Fruit-e O's	1 cup	4.0	113	9*
Health Valley Oat Bran Graham Crackers	6 (1 oz.)	3.6	86	10
General Mills Oatmeal Raisin Crisp	½ cup	3.0	110	12
Health Valley Oat Bran Animal Cookies	7 (1 oz.)	2.6	90	13
Continental Oatmeal Goodness Bread	1 sl. (1.3 oz.)	2.3	90	15*
For Comparison				
Beans, lentils, split peas	½ cup, cooked	—	105-135	1

[1]All serving sizes for cereals are for one ounce, dry.

[2]Packets of instant oatmeal contain dried fruit and flavorings in addition to ⅓ cup oatmeal.

*If oatmeal and oat flour are found to have the same cholesterol-lowering ability as oat bran, it would take fewer servings of these foods to lower cholesterol by three percent.

✔These products give you the biggest bang for your bite—that is, the most oat bran for the least fat and fewest calories.

‡Reprinted from *Nutrition Action Healthletter*, which is available from the Center for Science in the Public Interest, 1501 16th Street, N.W., Washington, D.C. 20036, for $19.95 for 10 issues, copyright 1988.

The consensus seems to be that eating high-fat, high-cholesterol foods along with oat bran is counterproductive. You cannot expect the oat bran to cancel out the negative effects of those foods. All the scientific evidence suggests that to lower cholesterol and protect against heart disease, a diet should be low in fats and other cholesterol-heavy foods and high in soluble fibers such as oat bran.

Q: *I'm having trouble eating a whole cup of oat bran every day. Am I getting any benefit if I eat less?*

A: Yes, any amount of oat bran you eat will have some beneficial effect on your cholesterol level.

Q: *Does oat bran work best if your cholesterol is only slightly elevated?*

A: Not necessarily. The original oat bran studies involved patients who had highly elevated serum-cholesterol levels of 250 milligrams or more. People with levels that aren't that high may not see the same dramatic effect.

Q: *If my cholesterol levels are normal, should I avoid oat bran?*

A: No, but you don't have to concern yourself with trying to consume large quantities every day. If your blood-cholesterol levels are within the normal range, the best advice is to follow a moderately low-cholesterol diet, along the guidelines recommended by the American Heart Association (see Chapter 5), and include oats, as well as other whole grains, as a substantial part of your overall nutrition plan.

The Center for Science in the Public Interest cautions that estimating how much oat bran will lower cholesterol is not an exact science. Not only does the soluble fiber content of various foods and products vary, but individual responses vary as well. Best results are obtained when you can find a variety of ways to get soluble fiber into your diet.

In addition to oat bran, there are many other foods involved in a cholesterol-lowering diet. Eating only one or two foods in large amounts and excluding others can be harmful, even if those one or two are good for you. Researchers stress that a balanced diet, relatively low in saturated fats and cholesterol, is the best dietary strategy against heart disease. At the same time, they are closely watching certain foods that appear to be especially helpful when it comes to lowering cholesterol. Apples, barley, carrots, eggplant, olive oil, and certain fish and seafood are among these.

The following chapter looks at some of the basic guidelines for reducing cholesterol across your dietary spectrum.

5

Other Foods That Help Lower Cholesterol

Oat bran is not the only cholesterol "helper." Many foods can work the same way that oat bran and cholesterol-lowering drugs do—by washing away bile acids containing cholesterol in the intestinal tract or by curbing the liver's production of destructive LDL cholesterol.

Foods can be easily divided into those that raise cholesterol, those that have no effect on cholesterol, and those—like oat bran—that actually work in the body to carry away cholesterol. While oat bran is the best source, other foods also provide large quantities of soluble fiber: beans are especially good, and other legumes such as lentils are also high in valuable fiber. Further, oat bran, like all cholesterol-lowering agents, including drugs, is most effective when it is consumed in conjunction with a low-fat, low-cholesterol, high-fiber diet.

The object of any cholesterol-lowering diet is to incorporate the many foods that are themselves low in cholesterol and saturated fat, along with foods that can actually reduce cholesterol in the blood. These include skim and low-fat dairy products, grains, fruits and vegetables, dried beans and peas, fish, olive oil, and polyunsaturated vegetable oil.

Q: *What is the worst food in terms of blood cholesterol?*

A: The kinds and amounts of fats in the diet are more important than how much cholesterol you eat. Cholesterol is a fatty alcohol, but it is not the same as fat. Highly saturated dietary fats, like those in meat and butter, can raise blood cholesterol more than foods high in cholesterol.

Q: *How much fat is safe to consume?*

A: Current surveys show that Americans consume 37 percent of their calories in the form of fat, nearly half of it saturated. Most nutrition experts would like to see that percentage reduced to 30 percent of total calories. Here are the recommendations from the American Heart Association for lowering cholesterol and fats in the diet:

> *Cholesterol:* No more than 300 milligrams daily
> *Carbohydrates:* 50 percent of daily calories
> *Protein:* 20 percent of daily calories
> *Fats:* 30 percent of daily calories, divided as follows:
> 10% from saturated fat;
> 10% from polyunsaturated fat;
> 10% from monosaturated fat.

If blood cholesterol does not respond to these alterations, these levels can be lowered to 200 milligrams of cholesterol daily and no more than 20 percent of calories from fat.

Q: *Do any foods contain HDL cholesterol?*

A: No. You cannot directly eat HDL cholesterol, but various foods can help increase the relative amount circulating in your blood. Among them are fatty fish and shellfish. Also effective are monounsaturated vegetable oil, such as olive, canola, and peanut oils, as well as foods containing other soluble fibers, such as apples and dried beans and peas.

Q: *What foods lower LDL cholesterol?*

A: Polyunsaturated vegetable oils like corn, soybean, safflower, sunflower, and cottonseed lower total blood cholesterol, including LDL and, to some extent, the beneficial HDL.

Q: *What are the major foods to avoid?*

A: Foods that are high in either cholesterol or saturated fat and can raise levels of cholesterol in the blood. Foods to avoid include egg yolks and organ meats. Sausage and cold cuts. Hard and soft cheeses and cream cheese. Butter, cream, lard, vegetable shortening, beef and poultry fat, and coconut, palm kernel, and palm oils.

Q: *What is the benefit of omega-3 fatty acids?*

A: Omega-3 fatty acids can help lower LDL levels and raise HDL.

Q: *I'm confused about fish—which kind is good and which kind is bad?*

A: Nearly all fish and seafood are good cholesterol fighters. Best are cold saltwater fishes such as salmon, tuna, herring, and mackerel. Canned tuna is slightly richer in fish oil if it is packed in water, not soybean oil. Freshwater fish and fish raised in tanks or ponds are not as beneficial as these "fatty" saltwater fishes.

Seafood like clams and shrimp and crab are relatively high in cholesterol, but they can actually lower LDL cholesterol because the fat they contain is rich in omega-3s. Sardines and anchovies are also high in cholesterol but rich in omega-3s. Buy them packed in water or drain the oil thoroughly.

Fish eggs are the things to avoid: stay away from caviar and shad roe, which are almost pure cholesterol.

Q: *What's the difference between saturated and unsaturated fats?*

A: For the most part saturated fats are derived from animal foods, and they tend to boost blood cholesterol by stimulating the liver's production of LDL. Saturated fats are solid at room temperature. They are found in meat and dairy foods, as well as in some plant products, specifically palm and coconut oils. It's important to know that saturated fats are not essential in the human diet.

> *Saturated Fats*
> Beef fat
> Butter
> Sweet cream
> Sour cream
> Lard
> Suet
> Cocoa butter
> Coconut oil
> Palm oil
> Palm kernel oil
> Hydrogenated oil
> Shortening
> Whole milk
> Whole milk cheese

Unsaturated fats are liquid at room temperature. These are the fats that help lower LDL cholesterol.

Here's how the different fats break down:

> *Monounsaturated Fats*
> Peanut oil
> Olive oil
> Canola oil
>
> *Polyunsaturated Fats*
> Corn oil
> Cottonseed oil
> Safflower oil

Sesame oil
Soybean oil
Sunflower oil

Q: *There's a lot of confusion about polyunsaturated fats and monounsaturated fats. Which is better in terms of lowering cholesterol?*

A: A decade ago, it was believed that only polyunsaturated fats would lower cholesterol. New experiments in animals indicate that polyunsaturates tend to suppress the immune system. Monounsaturates, which also reduce total cholesterol, are now preferred. The most prominent monounsaturates are peanut and olive oils.

The traditional Mediterranean diet, rich in fish, grains, fruits, vegetables, and olive oil, is regarded as a healthy alternative to such high cholesterol foods as red meat, eggs, and wholemilk dairy products. Much of the fat in this regional fare comes from the monounsaturates in olive oil, which may explain why southern Italians, for example, have one of the lowest heartdisease rates in the Western hemisphere—even though their HDL levels are significantly below average. They appear to be protected by their low LDL counts, which they owe to a diet relatively low in saturated fat.

Q: *On some packaged foods I see something called "palmitate" or "palmitic acid" on the label. I assume this is a saturated tropical oil, but I'm not sure.*

A: Yes, it is tropical oil. Palmitic acid is used to put vitamin A, a fat-soluble vitamin, into the food. But the amount used is so small that it is of no concern, even to those on restricted low-fat diets.

Q: *I've heard the erucic acid vegetable oil is dangerous. Isn't this an ingredient in canola oil, which is supposed to be so good for you?*

A: Canola oil and rapeseed oil have even less saturated fat than safflower and sunflower oils. Erucic acid vegetable oil is a component of these beneficial oils, however, and may cause liver damage. A technique to remove much of the acid makes it possible to use these oils, and only canola oils that are low in erucic acid may be sold in this country. But check the label to make sure it reads "low erucic acid."

Q: *Should I avoid dairy products if I want to reduce risk of heart disease?*

A: No, but choose the low-fat or skim-milk versions, and stay away from most cheese. Even hard cheeses are high in cholesterol-raising saturated fat and rich in cholesterol. In fact, cheese is higher in saturated fat than most lean meats.

Cream cheese gets 85 percent of its calories from the fat, and the typical serving is much larger than that of butter. Curd cheeses, such as low-fat cottage cheese, farmer's cheese, and pot cheese, and low-fat yogurts are much better.

Q: *Is buttermilk good for a low-fat diet?*

A: Buttermilk is equal in calories and fat to whole milk. The thickness comes from adding culture to milk. Low-fat buttermilk has only 1 percent fat, and could be used in moderation in a cholesterol-lowering diet.

Q: *Are nondairy creamers and nondairy whipped toppings better than those made from real milk and cream?*

A: Not as a rule. Some nondairy creamers, either powdered or liquid, contain coconut oil, even though they boast "no cholesterol." Read the label carefully before buying these products.

Q: *Are products made with soybeans beneficial for cholesterol?*

A: Yes. Soybean products such as tofu can have a dramatic impact on people with high blood cholesterol. In one European study, soy proteins actually counteracted the effects of a high-fat diet, and soy products are highly recommended in a cholesterol-lowering plan.

Q: *What about red meat?*
A: Lean meats in moderate quantities are acceptable. But organ meats, such as liver and kidneys, contain large amounts of cholesterol and should be avoided.

Q: *What is the controversy about niacin?*
A: Niacin is a B vitamin that is important for metabolism of carbohydrates, fats, and protein in all cells, and also for the functioning of the nervous system. Niacin supposedly lowers LDL and increases HDL. Niacin received wide attention because science writer Robert Kowalski, author of *The Eight-Week Cholesterol Cure*, effectively incorporated it into his personal plan to reduce his own cholesterol.

Many researchers have been alarmed over the recommendation to consume large quantities of niacin because an excess may produce such side effects as gastric upset and heart arrhythmias. Anyone with liver damage or gout shouldn't take niacin at all. Niacin should be considered a drug and taken only under a doctor's supervision. The U.S. Recommended Daily Allowance is 20 milligrams a day.

Q: *What foods naturally contain niacin?*
A: Liver, tuna, salmon, swordfish, poultry, peanuts, and whole grains. All except liver are recommended as part of a cholesterol-lowering dietary plan. Your body can also convert the amino acid tryptophan, found in milk and eggs, to niacin. Niacin is soluble in hot water and alcohol, but

may be destroyed by ordinary cooking methods. If stewing or braising poultry or meats, save and consume cooking liquid.

Q: *Why are some vegetable oils that do not contain cholesterol considered dangerous?*

A: Even though some plants used to make oil do not contain cholesterol, they may contain saturated fats. Coconut oil, palm kernel oil, and palm oil, which are widely used in processed foods, raise cholesterol in the blood, even though they do not contain cholesterol. A product may be correctly labeled as "cholesterol free" but still contain a large amount of cholesterol-raising saturated fat. These oils have the same destructive effect on arteries as animal fats, even though their labels proclaim "no cholesterol."

Q: *I've heard that chocolate is one of the worst foods you can eat. Besides the obvious reason that candy contains large amounts of sugar, why is chocolate so bad?*

A: Chocolate contains *two* fatty acids. One is palmitic acid, a highly saturated tropical vegetable oil that raises cholesterol. The other is stearic acid, found in the fat of red meat and cocoa butter. New evidence shows, however, that stearic acid does not raise LDL cholesterol and probably is not as bad as everyone thought. But until someone figures out how to make chocolate bars without tropical oils, chocolate candy is high on the list of foods to avoid.

Q: *What is stearic acid? Is it good for you or bad for you?*

A: A new study from Dr. Scott M. Grundy and Dr. Andrea Bonanome at the University of Texas at Dallas has shown that stearic acid, a saturated fat, actually has a tendency to lower cholesterol levels. Stearic acid is found in cocoa butter and beef fat. But while stearic acid may be good for you, it usually goes hand in hand with palmitic acid, also found in chocolate and beef, which clearly raises cholesterol. Dr. Grundy has said that the study indicates that moderate portions of lean beef are acceptable, even on a low-cholesterol diet. So while the news about stearic acid is good, it's not so good that we should begin consuming large amounts of red meat and chocolate candy.

Q: *I've heard that chicken is just as bad, when it comes to fat content, as red meat. Is this true?*

A: It's true. If you eat poultry without first removing the skin you might as well eat a sirloin steak.

Q: *I've heard that wheat bread is no better than white bread when it comes to fiber content. Is this true?*

A: Yes. The word "wheat" on a label of dark-colored bread suggests that the bread is made from whole wheat, which may not be the case. (White bread is also made from wheat.) The dark color may come from caramel coloring. Only bread labeled 100 percent whole wheat is made from whole grain and has a significant fiber content.

Best Choices for a Low-Fat, Low-Cholesterol Diet

All raw or steamed vegetables, including broccoli, brussels sprouts, carrots, celery, corn, parsnips, squash, and turnips
All green, leafy vegetables, including cabbage, collards, kale, lettuce, and spinach
All fresh fruits, including berries and melons
Dried beans of all varieties
Dried peas of all varieties
Lentils
Potatoes, white and sweet

Pasta

Brown rice

Whole grains and cereals of all kinds

100 percent whole-wheat bread

Pita bread

Sauces made with tomatoes or other vegetables, wine, fish and seafood stocks, or chicken broth

Soups made with broth, vegetables, noodles, grains, beans, or fish

Fish, all varieties, broiled or poached

Seafood

Poultry, without skin or fat, including chicken, turkey, and cornish hen

Garlic, onions, herbs and spices can add flavor and zest to dishes that do not include butter, cream, or salt.

Foods to Avoid in a Low-Fat, Low-Cholesterol Diet

Duck and goose

Luncheon meats

Corned beef

Spareribs, ground pork, and pork sausage

Ground meat, including ground veal and ground lamb patties, and chopped steak made from chuck

Fried foods, including fried vegetables and fish

Breaded coatings

Gravies

Butter, oil, and cheese sauces

Cream and cheese sauces

Hard and soft cheeses

Nondairy cheese substitutes

Sour cream and creamy dips

Mayonnaise
Creamy salad dressings
Tartar sauce
Mousses
Pâté
Creamed soups
Biscuits
Croissants
Most commercial muffins
Butter rolls
Cake
Pies
Ice cream
Whipped cream
Puddings
Custards
Nondairy milk substitutes

Tips for a Low-Fat, Low-Cholesterol Diet

The idea behind reducing blood cholesterol is to *reduce*, not eliminate, dietary fats and cholesterol in the diet and to increase complex carbohydrates. Here are some suggestions:

- If a product contains fat or oil, make sure it is a polyunsaturated or monounsaturated fat or oil that helps lower blood cholesterol.
- If you eat meat, choose lean cuts of red meat, veal chops and roast veal, or pork tenderloin.
- Trim excess fat from red meats before cooking. Remove skin from poultry before or after cooking.
- Use cooking methods that help remove fat such as broiling (without butter), poaching, baking, steaming, roasting, or braising.
- Avoid fatty cuts of beef, pork, and lamb. Prime meats have more marbling than other meats. Lamb patties and chopped steak made from ground

chuck also have a high fat content. Ground round is a better choice, or extra lean ground sirloin.

- Use liquid vegetable oils and margarine high in polyunsaturated or monounsaturated fats.
- Avoid oils and nondairy products that contain palm, palm kernel, and coconut oil.
- Stay away from fatty luncheon meats.
- Avoid cream sauces, hollandaise, béarnaise, cheese sauces, and butter sauces.
- Marinate skinless chicken and fish in lemon or lime juice, wine, broth, tomato juice, or low-fat yogurt rather than oil to keep calories to a minimum.
- Don't chop, peel, tear, or shell vegetables until they are ready to be cooked. Bruised vegetables rapidly lose nutritional value when surfaces are exposed to air.
- Cook vegetables with their skins on, even if you're going to remove the skins before serving.
- Retain and use the coarse outer leaves of lettuce and broccoli; they have more vitamins and minerals than the inside leaves.
- Cook fresh vegetables as little as possible. Vegetables that are cooked least retain the most nutrients.
- Rather than soaking dried peas and beans overnight, boil them in water for two minutes, then allow them to stand for an hour before cooking. Prolonged soaking leaches vitamins.
- Do not rinse rice or pasta before or after cooking. Rinsing washes away many of the valuable vitamins and minerals.
- Always measure and use the proper amounts of water required to cook rice and other grains. Many nutrients are lost if excess cooking water must be poured off.
- When offered a choice, opt for whole fresh fruit rather than freshly squeezed fruit juice. Whole fresh fruit is more nutritious, because the nutrients and fiber are retained in the pulp.
- Reduce fats in recipes by cutting back on amounts called for by at least one-third. If a dish seems too

dry, add broth, wine, or even fruit juice.

- Use a vegetable spray to coat pans.
- Use low-fat dairy products in place of those made with whole milk or cream. Low-fat yogurt, or low-fat cottage cheese blended with yogurt or skim milk, can be substituted for sour cream.
- Use broth in place of butter to sauté onions and vegetables.
- Instead of using fat plus flour, cold skim milk or stock can be blended with finely ground oat bran to make a smooth paste for sauces and gravies.
- Skim fat from soup stock, pasta sauces, chili, and casseroles.
- Use skim milk or cooking broth to mash potatoes (instead of milk and butter).
- Replace mayonnaise, margarine, and salad dressing with the low-fat, water-whipped varieties. The key to using these products is to recognize that they have a substantial water content, which means under heat they do not always behave in the same way as the original product. In general, these products are excellent substitutes in grain and vegetable dishes, and in casseroles. In baked goods, however, they may not substitute exactly. Experiment with the best combinations of low-fat and regular products.
- Thicken "creamy" soups with pureed vegetables and low-fat dry milk instead of cream.
- Substitute egg whites for whole eggs. If a one-for-one doesn't work well, you can still use more egg whites and fewer egg yolks.

Maintaining a Low-Fat, Low-Cholesterol Diet in Restaurants

In the last few decades the American way of eating has undergone a profound change. One-third of our meals are consumed outside the home; when we do eat at home, we often resort to take-out gourmet or fast foods. Dining out in any sense of the word means that most of us will have to work harder to maintain low-fat, low-cholesterol diets.

Most restaurants, even the most sophisticated ones, still prepare foods with the same high-fat ingredients. Butter and cream may be present in large quantities; prime cut meats may be sautéed or fried, vegetables are sauced with everything from butter to béarnaise. Desserts are richer than ever. With the notable exception of Japanese or seafood restaurants, fats, cholesterol, sugar, and salt seem to be the staples of the day.

Yet diners well versed in nutrition can find selections in virtually any restaurant. The goal is to select meals that are low or moderate in calories, fat, and cholesterol—and high in pleasure and entertainment—even when you don't know the ingredients in a dish or exactly how it is prepared.

You'll get the best results from restaurants that cook to order. Some dishes, however, cannot be made without specific ingredients (a hollandaise sauce cannot be made without the eggs). So even in restaurants where every dish is individually prepared, there are limitations to what you can ask for.

Restaurants that serve mostly prepared-in-advance foods will find it more difficult to alter the contents of dishes. Even here, though, you can ask for sauces and salad dressings to be served on the side.

Rather than asking a lot of questions about how certain dishes are cooked, bone up on cooking basics. An experienced cook, or even a well-read noncook, will know without asking what various sauces are:

Béchamel, béarnaise, and hollandaise are made of the same high-cholesterol ingredients, whether they're made at home or in a restaurant.

Thousand Island and Creamy Italian salad dressings are always the same high-fat dressings, no matter where they are made.

"Sautéed" always means cooked in butter. If food is fried, it doesn't matter what it's fried in—it will be high in calories.

When you have a special request, make it directly. Rather than asking whether the chef uses butter on the broiled fish, make a statement: "I'd like the fish broiled 'dry' without butter or margarine." It's more efficient for the waiter, who may know very little about how the chef cooks, and you're more likely to get what you want.

Always order "à la carte." Extras that come with a meal are hard to pass up once they're in front of you.

More important than what is ordered is *how* it's prepared. Cream sauces, cheese sauces, butter sauces, and the generic "gravy" are all high in fat and cholesterol. Any food that is creamed, panfried, "crispy," or sautéed is also high in calories, fat, and cholesterol.

Restaurant-made casseroles, hashes, and pot pies are also likely to have elevated levels of fat and cholesterol. Even a vegetable casserole may be loaded with cheese or cream.

As a general rule, the simpler preparations are the best in terms of low-fat cooking. Choose entrées that are broiled ("dry" or with lemon or wine), poached, baked, steamed, roasted, or braised. These designations do not necessarily mean that no butter or oil is used. You will need to make a special request if you want butter or oil to be eliminated entirely. Although tomato and wine-based sauces also may be made with some butter or oil, these sauces are generally much lower in fat than cream-based sauces.

Chefs cannot always alter a dish to suit a specific request—either the dish itself will not adapt to a change of ingredients or it has been prepared in advance. For this reason, it's always a good idea to request that sauces and salad dressings be served "on the side." This is the single most important request you can make, and one that can usually be obliged in every restaurant. Sauces served on the side mean that you can judge for yourself the amount to pour on your food. In most cases, a little bit of sauce or dressing tastes as good as a lot.

Many dessert lovers can satisfy a sweet tooth with a dish of sherbet, or sorbet. Although sugary, it does not usually contain fat and is a better choice than pudding, cake, or pie. Angel food cake, if available, is another low-cholesterol choice because it is made with egg whites rather than whole eggs. Fresh berries or any other fresh fruit, minus the cream or egg-heavy zabaglione sauce, is a classic nonfat answer for those who crave something sweet.

Dining out should always be enjoyable and a little special, even for those who do it every day. Get in the habit of asking for low-fat dairy products and foods prepared without fats. Even if the restaurant is unable to oblige a special request, eventually they start to get the message that customers are interested in healthful foods. It wasn't long ago that only a few restaurants served brewed decaffeinated coffee, but today diners can find it almost everywhere. Consumers can influence what restaurants offer; the more often you ask, the more likely it is that low-fat, low-cholesterol foods will begin to appear regularly on restaurant menus.

Perhaps the best knowledge a health-conscious consumer can have is knowing how to shop. Americans are fortunate to have such an astonishing variety of produce and packaged goods to choose from, but this abundance has led to many problems when it comes to selecting those foods that offer quality nutrition. This has become particularly evident when it comes to choosing oat bran products.

6

Supermarket Shopping

Oat cereal? Oat bread? What is the reality of the packaged-food industry's rush to fill a new demand for cholesterol-lowering foods by introducing oats into many different kinds of products? If you are shopping for foods low in fats and cholesterol, how can you easily distinguish which to buy and which to avoid?

Labels can be deceptive. Some products that blatantly advertise "no cholesterol" use highly saturated fats such as coconut, palm, and palm kernel oils, none of which have "cholesterol," but all of which are known to be dangerous when it comes to building atherosclerosis.

On the other hand, some manufacturers are beginning to replace highly saturated fats in their products with healthier polyunsaturated or mono-unsaturated oils. For example, Cracklin' Oat Bran used to contain coconut oil, along with oat bran. But now a reformulated product has begun to appear on the supermarket shelves, its high-saturated coconut oil replaced by unsaturated vegetable oil.

Kellogg, Sunshine Biscuits, RJR Nabisco, General Mills, and General Foods are also finding ways to eliminate tropical oils, beef tallow, and lard from their products. Sunshine Biscuits recently issued a statement announcing that it was "committed to eliminating all use of palm oil and palm kernel in its cookie and cracker products." In addition, it said it had already removed coconut oil from its products. Nabisco Brands has said of the twenty-four new products it introduced last year, only two contain tropical oils. Both of these products are chocolate cookies. Kellogg is concentrating on getting the highly saturated fats out of its cereals.

Why do some manufacturers continue to use "bad" oils, even when they know better? For one thing, the manufacturers say that consumer surveys show that the product tastes better. Certain oils also may give the product a longer shelf life. And there is always the question of cost. Tropical oils tend to be less expensive than other vegetable oils like soybean, corn, cottonseed or canola.

The Food and Drug Administration believes that the case against tropical oils may have been overstated, saying that in the overall fat-laden American diet these oils are relatively minor contributors. Dr. Michael Jacobson, the executive director of the Center for Science in the Public Interest, agrees that tropical oils play a modest role. Red meat and dairy products are considered more worrisome, but at the same time Dr. Jacobson says, "It doesn't make sense for a manufacturer to use these cholesterol-raising fats when safer ones are available."

While all of this change is taking place, consumers still need to search out and carefully select healthful products. Existing federal regulations do not protect consumers against factual, but misleading, labeling. For example, products have been known to claim that they provide "more iron than milk," without noting that milk actually contains very little iron. One packager boasted "no preservatives added" on a package of raisins, without adding that raisins don't need preservatives.

The Food and Drug Administration has said it

will not challenge manufacturers making "reasonably accurate claims," a term it has yet to define. Federal Trade Commission regulations allow a manufacturer to make health claims as long as they are substantiated by one or two scientific studies—even if other equally convincing studies contradict the claim.

What all this adds up to is that if you are concerned about your intake of saturated fats, your best defense is becoming a skilled label reader. It is by no means a perfect art because labels do not have to tell you much of anything, but you can concentrate on buying those products that voluntarily give you the information you need.

Intelligent shopping requires careful analysis, particularly of the information regarding fat content. Most labels measure fat content by weight, but nutrition experts recommend working out the percentage of total calories that come from fat. For example, a 1-ounce serving of a cheese with a label that proclaims "reduced fat" may indeed be only one-quarter fat by weight, but it may be 80 percent fat in terms of calories.

When shopping, remember to stop by the health food store. Although many items are more costly in health food stores, these stores can be an excellent source of bulk foods such as bran, brown rice, and other grains and cereals. Many of these items are now available in supermarkets, but health food stores have a much wider selection of products, and you won't have to pay for excess packaging. Compare the price of beans, grains, cereal, dried fruit, nuts, oils, and spices.

Q: *Why are labels so confusing? Aren't there laws to keep them in line?*

A: Yes, plenty of them. The Food and Drug Administration (FDA), the United States Department of Agriculture (USDA), and the Federal Trade Commission (FTC) are all involved in setting standards for labeling, grading, and selling various foods. In general, the FDA is responsible for food labeling except on meat and poultry, which is governed by the USDA. And the FTC is the watchdog on advertising. However, these agencies often overlap to the point where information is confusing or misleading.

While progress has been made, it is still not easy to tell exactly what a product has to offer in terms of fat and cholesterol. Nevertheless, you can tell a lot about the contents and nutritional value of a product if you know the legal meaning of commonly used nutritional phrases and the limitations on health claims.

Q: *Some labels have a lot of nutrition information, and others don't seem to have any at all. What must a label include?*

A: FDA regulations require manufacturers of all products to furnish the following information on food labels:

- Name of the food.
- Style and variety of the food.
- A list of ingredients in descending order by weight. The ingredient statement is the single most accurate source of information about the contents of any food package. But labels do not have to indicate how much of any particular ingredient the product contains.
- Additives, including preservatives, must be specifically named, but color, flavors, and spices need only be described as "artificial color," "artificial flavor" or "natural flavor."
- If the label includes a picture, it must resemble the contents.
- Any special dietary properties, such as "fortified" or "low salt."
- Net contents or net weight, including packing fluid.
- Name and address of packer, manufacturer, or distributor.

That's the basic labeling requirement—except when a nutrient is added or when the manufacturer makes a specific nutritional claim for a product. Then that product must contain a nutrition label, which has much more of the information that you need than a standard label.

Q: *Why are nutrition labels so helpful?*
A: About half of the processed foods currently on the market must supply nutritional information. Many manufacturers, in response to consumer demand, also voluntarily provide nutrition labels.

Nutrition information on food labels can help consumers choose foods with less fat and cholesterol, but it is important to compare similar products before buying. Many manufacturers reduce the serving size—and sometimes the size of the package—by a few ounces to make it appear that the product has fewer calories. Serving sizes often vary from brand to brand or product to product. Consumers should also be aware that a calorie count may have an error factor of plus or minus 20 percent. 130 calories per serving could mean anywhere from 104 to 156 calories.

A nutrition label must contain the following information:

- Serving size, based on what an average adult male engaged in light physical activity ordinarily consumes as part of a meal.
- Number of servings per package.
- Number of calories per serving.
- Number of grams of protein, carbohydrate, and fat.
- Sodium content in milligrams per serving.
- Per serving percentages of U.S. Recommended Daily Allowances for protein, vitamin A, vitamin C, thiamine, riboflavin, niacin, calcium, and iron. (Listing of other nutrients is optional.)

- Cholesterol information is optional, as is a breakdown of saturated and unsaturated fats, and the sugar, starch, and fiber composition of carbohydrates.
- When two foods are commonly eaten together, such as cereal with milk, nutritional information for the combination may also be included.

The "optional" information about fats, cholesterol, sugars, and carbohydrates may be the very information the consumer is looking for, yet it is not legally required. Search out the products that voluntarily provide such detailed information.

Q: *What's the difference between "light" and "lite"?*

A: These words, and their spellings, are almost meaningless as far as nutritional information is concerned. They may mean that a food contains fewer calories, less fat, less sodium, or simply has a lighter color. To learn the significance of a "light" or "lite" food, you must read the label and also make a side-by-side comparison with a "regular" product. For a few products, however, "light" does have a specific meaning:

- Light cream must contain between 18 and 30 percent milk fat.
- Canned fruit in light syrup is made with less sugar, and the syrup is generally less dense than regular syrup.
- Light beer usually contains about one-third fewer calories than the standard version from the same brewery.
- Light salt means that potassium has replaced some of the sodium.
- Light meat and poultry products must contain 25 percent less fat than regular USDA standards; or at least 25 percent less fat, sodium, breading, or calories than the conventional

product. The label must indicate where the reduction can be found.

Q: *If a label says high in polyunsaturates, does it mean it is good for low-cholesterol diets?*

A: Not necessarily. A label does not have to provide the ratio of polyunsaturated to saturated fats. Therefore, the term "high in polyunsaturates" is only reliable if you know the ratio of polyunsaturates to saturates is at least 2:1.

Q: *If a label says "no cholesterol," can we assume it is good for low-cholesterol diets?*

A: No. Any product made with vegetable oil is likely to have "no cholesterol" on it. But it's no guarantee that the product is low in saturated fats. Check the ingredients list for coconut and palm oil. Both are highly saturated and neither contains cholesterol.

Q: *What does "imitation" mean? Does it mean that it is better or worse than the real thing?*

A: Usually worse, unless it's formulated for people with specific allergic reactions. Imitations are often cheaper than the regular product but usually nutritionally inferior.

A product that contains less protein, vitamins, or minerals than federally specified for its standard counterpart must be labeled "imitation." Dairy foods, juices, and processed meats are the three categories of food where imitations are likely to be found.

Foods lower in calories, fat, or cholesterol are not considered imitation.

Q: *What's the difference between "imitation" and "substitute"?*

A: When a food is nutritionally equivalent to a standard product, it may be called a "substitute" or it may be given a name that suggests the similarity.

The best example of this is Eggbeaters™ which contains no egg yolks. Because they are made from egg whites, however, Eggbeaters™ is entitled to use the word "egg."

Q: *What's the difference between "low calorie" and "reduced calorie"?*

A: "Low calorie" applies only to food with fewer than 40 calories per serving. The term cannot precede foods normally low in calories—no "low-calorie carrots" allowed.

"Reduced calorie" applies only to foods that contain one-third less than the standard product. The label must indicate the product to which it is being compared.

This is a tricky one, though. "Reduced calorie" does not automatically mean that a product has less cholesterol. "Reduced calorie" mayonnaise, for example, has about half the calories per tablespoon that regular mayonnaise has, but *may contain exactly the same amount of cholesterol*.

Q: *Exactly what does "dietetic" mean?*

A: "Dietetic" has two different meanings, and both of them are legal. Low- or reduced-calorie products can be labeled "dietetic."

The term also can be used when an item is designed for restricted diets. Dietetic cookies, for example, may be low only in sodium, not in calories. The label must indicate what is "dietetic" about a product.

Q: *Does "natural" have any real meaning?*

A: No, but it has many implications. The Federal Trade Commission has said that "natural" implies that a food has no preservatives, additives, or emulsifiers, or it may suggest that food has not been highly processed. However, a food may be "minimally processed" and still have been washed, peeled, ground, baked, roasted, aged, homogenized, canned, or bottled. So even in the context of the FTC's guidelines, "natural" has little solid definition, and it need not have any meaning at all.

There is an exception: Meat or poultry, governed by the USDA, can be labeled "natural" only if it contains no preservatives, artificial flavors, or colors.

Q: *What is the distinction between "lean" and "low fat" in meat labeling?*

A: USDA regulations govern claims for the fat content of meat and poultry. When such specific claims are made, the packager is required to specify actual percentages of fat:

- Lean or Low fat: The product may contain no more than 10 percent fat.
- Extra lean: Restricted to products containing no more than 5 percent fat.
- Light, Leaner, or Less fat: Used for meat products with 25 percent less fat than USDA standards specify. Light may also refer to a 25 percent reduction in breading, sodium, or calories, and the label must indicate what was reduced.

Q: *I am dizzy from reading cereal labels—are there any shortcuts to figuring out which ones offer the most fiber?*

A: Stick to the basic guidelines. Whole-grain cereals invariably are more nutritious: check to see if whole grains are the first item on a cereal's ingredients list. Cereals that require cooking— oat bran, rolled oats, toasted wheat, and cream of rice—usually have all the vitamins and fiber of the natural grain intact.

Q: *What other grains besides oats are good for low-fat, low-cholesterol diets?*

A: All of them. Brown rice is more nutritious than

polished white rice, and white rice is better than converted white rice. Instant white rice is at the lowest end of the fiber-nutrient scale. You can try bulgur, or cracked wheat, couscous, wheat berries, and many other grains available at health food stores and supermarkets. Be adventurous and experiment with new recipes.

Q: *Is nonfat dry milk all right in place of regular skim milk?*
A: Yes, nonfat dry milk contains equal amounts of nutrients, but is less costly than regular skim milk. Nonfat dry milk is excellent for cooking. You can also mix nonfat dry milk with skim milk and get a fuller-flavored milk.

Q: *How does condensed milk compare with regular milk?*
A: Condensed or evaporated milk has been heated and concentrated to remove 60 percent of the water. It contains at least 7.5 percent milkfat. Sweetened evaporated milk is much higher in calories than regular condensed milk because it must contain at least 8 percent milkfat and enough sweetener to prevent spoilage.

Q: *Is imitation milk all right for low-cholesterol diets?*
A: Imitation milk is used mostly for people allergic to milk. It is usually a blend of soy protein, corn syrup, coconut oil, vitamins and minerals, and as such is not especially recommended for those on low-cholesterol diets.

    Nondairy creamers, either powdered or liquid, may also contain coconut oil. When buying any imitation milk product, read the label carefully to make sure they do not contain tropical oils.

Q: *How does cheese stack up, in terms of fat?*
A: The lowest in fats and cholesterol are unripened

low-fat cottage, mozzarella, cream, and ricotta cheese. These cheeses can be eaten in limited amounts on a low-cholesterol diet. Ripened hard cheese—cheddar, Swiss, Muenster, and Parmesan—are high in fats. Processed cheese, cheese food, and cheese spread include thickeners, stabilizers, gums, and extra fat.

Q: *Is imitation cheese better than regular cheese when it comes to a low-cholesterol diet?*

A: No, it may be worse. Imitation cheese is likely to be made with hydrogenated vegetable oils. It's easy to confuse these products with real cheese, because they are usually packaged alike, and they are usually side by side in the dairy case.

Q: *Which is the best polyunsaturated fat to use?*

A: Corn is a good all-purpose polyunsaturated oil, but safflower, soybean, peanut, sesame, and sunflower are also good. Each has a slightly different flavor.

In selecting margarines, beware of partially hydrogenated oils, which convert natural vegetable oils to saturated fats to solidify margarines and vegetable shortenings. If it's solid at room temperature, it's saturated.

Liquid margarines and "soft" margarines are less hydrogenated, and therefore less saturated, than solid margarine. Always check the ratio of polyunsaturated to saturated fats on the labels, and try for 3:1.

Q: *I've noticed that many products list a lot of different oils on the package and say that the product might contain one or more of them. What are you supposed to do—guess?*

A: In marketing lingo it's called "flexi labeling," and it is a signal for consumers to pass it up. There is no way for anyone to know which oil has been used. A product whose label reads:

"Contains one of the following oils: corn, sun-flower, or coconut" is most likely to contain highly saturated coconut oil simply because it is the cheapest. The best advice is to stay clear of the product.

7

The Oat Bran Kitchen

Glory has been slow in coming to the humble oat. In ancient times wild oats were more of a nuisance than a food and forced themselves upon the attention of European farmers by invading their fields of wheat and barley like weeds. The story is told that cattle were observed one day eating oats that had been pulled from the fields and stacked up for burning. This gave their proprietor the idea of feeding the oats to livestock. For ages, thereafter, oats were thought fit only for consumption by horses and cows. In medieval times some humans began eating them, possibly because the oats strangled the wheat crop, forcing farmers to harvest the oats instead. Oats were classified in that time as a "coarse" food, which supposedly led to a coarsened character.

Eventually, however, oats were cultivated throughout central Europe, and reached Britain sometime during the Iron Age. The Scots became among the biggest oat-eaters, which brought ridicule from Dr. Johnson, who defined the oat as "a grain which in England is generally given to horses but in Scotland supports the people." If oatmeal ever caught on in America, *The New York Times* warned in the late 1800s, "the next generation of Americans will be as dyspeptic and Calvinistic as the majority of Scotsmen."

For all its bad notices, oatmeal did catch on. Its warming nutrition, its versatility, and its astonishing ability to thrive in soil too poor to support wheat and barley crops eventually made oats a staple in many countries around the world, including the United States. Back in the 1800s the Quaker Oats Company was purely a milling company; its oatmeal was the first breakfast cereal in the world to have a registered trademark.

In the early 1950s, American farmers were producing 1.3 billion bushels of oats a year for both human and livestock consumption. But again change was in the wind.

Modern technology had displaced the horses and mules that were big oats consumers. Science had taught farmers that other, cheaper feeds were better for cattle and hogs because they contained more carbohydrates to fatten them up. Another discouraging factor was a farm program that attracted farmers to crops that commanded higher subsidies than oats. Oat production began to fall, and over the next thirty year slid by 60 percent.

Even as production fell, there were signs that the oat would rise again. In the mid-1960s, researchers first identified the cholesterol-lowering properties of oats, and almost a dozen studies over the last eight years have confirmed it. As far as consumers are concerned, oats are making a big comeback, thanks almost solely to the news that oat bran can help lower cholesterol.

New oat products in the form of muffins, cookies, crackers, bread, and health bars turn up daily in the supermarkets. Some of these products are handsomely packaged imports, priced with commensurate inflation. Others are ordinary candy bars sprinkled with bits of oat bran.

The demand for oat bran by consumers is so great that suppliers can charge any price they want for it. A 16-ounce package of oat bran that cost 89 cents in

September 1988 cost more than twice that in January 1989. The 1988 drought, which baked the northern plains and devastated much of the nation's wheat, barley, and oat crop, also contributed to the escalating price of oat bran. On the commodity exchanges the price of a 32-pound bushel of oats soared to a record high of $3.18.

Supermarkets and health food stores are finding themselves periodically out of stock. Quaker Oats, which buys more than half of the nation's crop, and other processors cannot process it fast enough. Yet U.S. production remains low. The result is an increasing dependence on imports, primarily from Canada, Scandinavia, and Argentina.

The increased demand for oat products may put farmers in a frame of mind to consider raising their production. While oats still can't be sold for as much as wheat or corn, they don't cost as much to grow, either, because of modest fertilizer needs. Also in their favor, oats combat soil erosion, provide ground cover for other crops and are harvested in the summer when many farmers are in a lull before the big early-autumn push to get in other grains.

The oat bran muffin is now nationally famous, but it takes a lot of oat bran to deliver a supply sufficient to lower cholesterol. How do you get all the oats you need into your daily diet? Many people stop at the muffin and cereal stage and never go any further because they don't know how to add oats to the other foods that they eat every day. As a result, they eventually get bored with muffins and cereal and stop eating oat bran altogether.

It's much easier to stay with a low-cholesterol program and get the quantity of oat bran you need if you routinely incorporate oats in a variety of foods. You don't have to be a great chef to do it, and you don't have to be a prize-winning baker, or any kind of baker at all.

Oats or oat bran can be toasted, ground, sprouted, and used in the multitude of ways that you would any other grain products, from flour to wheat germ to barley to rice. It can be used as a replacement for bread crumbs and cracker crumbs. Oat bran can be sprinkled on top of and stirred into any number of dishes. Soups, stews, stuffings, breads, cereals easily incorporate oat bran.

There are a few tips that can help you begin using oat bran in your everyday cooking. For example, oat products tend to absorb a lot of liquid, even after they have finished cooking. That means that oats require a little more liquid than most grains. Nor does every manufacturer produce oat bran in a uniform size and texture. Variations in milling make different brands look a little different and behave differently from each other in the cooking process. Liquid will have to be adjusted to accommodate these differences.

Here are some common questions about muffins, breads, and many other foods you can make from oat bran.

Q: *Can you freeze oat bran muffins?*
A: Yes, they freeze very well, and this is the preferred method of storage. You can make one dozen or more at a time and freeze them immediately. The night before you want them, simply remove the muffins from the freezer and leave at room temperature; while muffins can be eaten without reheating, they are even better if put in the toaster oven for a couple of minutes. If muffins are removed from the freezer just before use, place them in a 300-degree oven for 15 minutes.

Q: *When I make oat bran muffins, I find they develop a musty odor in about 24 hours. Does this mean they've gone bad? Is there any way to prevent it?*
A: The qualities that make oat bran healthy also make it difficult to bake with. It is extremely absorbent, for one thing, which means that muf-

fins tend to become soggy or even moldy. If muffins aren't going to be eaten within 24 hours, it's best to refrigerate them or freeze them right away.

Q: *The oat bran muffins I make at home have a gritty texture. Is there some way to correct this?*

A: Many people complain about the texture of oat bran muffins, not realizing that they are not supposed to be like an ordinary muffin. Rather than being cakelike, oat bran muffins may be sticky, crunchy, or crumbly, depending on whether they contain honey, nuts, or raisins.

Instead of comparing oat bran muffins with regular muffins, you should compare them with a natural grain product. If you dislike the gritty quality of oat bran baked goods, try grinding the oat bran in a blender or food processor before using it.

You can also make a multigrain flour by combining whole rolled oats, oat bran, whole-wheat flour, corn meal, and white flour in nearly any proportions and grinding them together in the blender or food processor.

Q: *How many grams are there in one cup of oat bran?*

A: There are 85.2 grams.

Q: *I understand that oat bran won't rise. Is there any way to use it in yeast breads?*

A: Because neither oat bran nor oat flour has gluten, it cannot rise. However, it can be included in recipes for yeast bread simply by combining it with the flour from other grains. Oat bran can also be used as a substitute for part of the flour in pancakes and waffles.

Q: *Should I keep oat bran in the refrigerator?*

A: Whole oats and oat bran have a very long shelf life and don't need to be refrigerated. Baked goods and cereals made with oats keep even longer if refrigerated.

Q: *I am not interested in baking and dislike cooking in general. On the other hand, I'm getting a little tired of cereal. Are there any easy uncomplicated ways to use oat bran and whole oats besides cereal?*

A: You can sprinkle plain oat bran over almost anything you're eating—cottage cheese, peanut butter, soups, coleslaw, pasta sauce, strawberries, canned fruit, or nonfat yogurt.

If you can bear to cook just a little, you can toast whole rolled oats, steel-cut oats, or oat groats and eat them as snacks. Toasted oats have a crunchy, nutlike taste. You can substitute toasted oats for nuts, wheat germ, wheat bran, or bread crumbs. Sprinkle them on salads and on top of your cereal, sliced bananas, or applesauce.

You can toast oats simply by placing two cups on an unoiled cookie sheet and baking in a 350-degree oven for about 10 or 15 minutes, until lightly browned. Stir them several times while baking. You can also toast groats and steel-cut oats in a dry skillet over medium heat for five minutes, stirring frequently. Store toasted oats in a tightly covered container.

Q: *What are oat sprouts?*

A: Oat sprouts are another boost for those of us who don't like to cook. Sprouts can be tossed into a salad, added to soups or vegetables, or used in sandwiches. The only thing you have to do is help the oats to sprout, which is a noncooking technique that appeals to the gardener in most people.

Q: *How do you get an oat to sprout?*

A: The hardest part is finding a supply of *unhulled*

whole oats, which isn't always easy. You can try a health food store, but you will probably have better luck at a seed or feed supplier, which is fine if you live in the country but impossible if you are a city dweller. Ordinary oat groats or whole oats will not sprout because the outer husk has been removed.

Once you've obtained the unhulled whole oats, getting them to sprout is easier than it sounds. Here are the steps:

½ cup whole oats with their hulls intact
1 jar of warm water

Soak overnight. Drain, then fill the jar with fresh warm water, cover with cheesecloth, and snap a rubber band around it. Shake the jar hard, then drain the water off quickly. Lay the jar on its side inside a kitchen cabinet, and leave it alone. In the evening, and again in the morning, fill the jar with water, shake it, and drain. Return the jar to the cabinet. Continue this twice-a-day watering process until the shoots are as long as the original oats, usually within two to four days. Cut off the empty hulls before eating. One-half cup of whole oats turns into a whole cup of sprouts. Store sprouts in the refrigerator.

Q: *Is oat flour made from whole oats or from oat bran?*

A: Oat flour is milled from whole oats (groats). Sometimes it includes the bran—and sometimes it doesn't. Always check the label before purchasing packaged oat flour to make sure it is made from the whole oat *with the bran*.

Whole oat flour is just as nutritious as whole oats and can be used in place of wheat flour in almost any recipe, except those made with yeast. Pure oat products, whether they are oat bran or whole oats, cannot rise because oats do not contain gluten. People allergic to wheat flour can usually eat oat flour. If you cannot find packaged whole oat flour in your supermarket or health food store, it's easy to grind your own in a food processor from any kind of whole oat.

Q: *Why can't you make oat flour from pure oat bran?*

A: You can. Oat bran is already ground into fairly small flakes, but you can make it even more floury by running it through a blender or food processor. Use it just as you would oat flour.

Q: *Where do you get oat flour?*

A: You can buy oat flour in a health food store, or you can make your own in a food processor or blender from either rolled oats, steel-cut oats, or oat groats. To make one cup of flour requires 1¼ cups of whole oats.

Q: *How do you use oat flour in recipes?*

A: In recipes for baked goods you can substitute either oat flour or ground oat bran for up to one third of the all-purpose flour. Both can also be used for thickening, breading, baking, dredging, and browning. Do not sift oat flour before using it, as you may sift out all the bran.

Q: *Does oat flour taste different from regular flour when you use it in baked goods?*

A: Oat flour has a sweet scent and a nutlike taste. Breads made with oat flour tend to be denser, sweeter, and moister. Other baked goods are likely to be more crumbly in texture.

Q: *Do you have to be careful in the way you keep oat flour?*

A: No. Ground oat flour can be stored in airtight containers in cool dry locations for as long as six months.

Q: *Is there such a thing as packaged oat bran flour?*

A: Not yet. You probably will have to grind your own in a food processor or blender. Blend or process on "grind" or the highest speed until you get a fine, flourlike texture, usually about one minute.

Q: *Can I use oat bran in place of regular flour to make gravy?*

A: Yes. Finely ground oat bran can be used in much the same way as whole oat flour. You can use ground oat bran to thicken soups, gravy, sauce, stew, or puddings. Use the same amount of ground oat bran or whole oat flour as you would regular flour. Oat products are equally effective at thickening hot or cold liquids.

Q: *Can you use whole rolled oats in place of wheat flour?*

A: Yes, you don't have to grind oat bran or whole oats to use them as substitutes for flour. You can use oat products in stuffings and fillings, in ground meats like meat loaf. You can use them in place of bread crumbs in any recipe. You can also add toasted oats to almost anything where you would normally use bread crumbs, nuts, wheat bran, or wheat germ. When you do substitute oat products, however, make sure to add a little more liquid to the recipe.

Q: *How do you use oat groats?*

A: Oat groats are simply whole grains, and like all whole grains they are cooked in liquid until they are swollen and tender.

Rinse the groats in water and drain. Heat water or broth (the ratio of liquid to groats is 2 to 1), and add the groats. Stir and let liquid come back to boiling. Turn heat to low, and cover. Simmer groats slowly until they are tender and the cooking liquid has been absorbed. If the groats are not tender when the liquid has been absorbed, add more liquid and continue cooking. Cooking time: 45 minutes.

Q: *Can you just use plain oat bran for coatings in place of bread crumbs?*

A: Yes—dip skinless chicken, vegetables, fish into oat bran before baking, broiling, or sautéing. You can also season the oat bran with various herbs of your choice—basil, thyme, marjoram, tarragon, or rosemary—all will add a distinctive flavor to the bran, just as they do to bread crumbs.

Q: *What about oat breads you buy in the store—are these a good source of oat bran?*

A: Check ingredients list and see what comes first. For example, one bread product that is called "OAT BREAD" in very large letters, lists oats as the fifth ingredient, after flour, honey, molasses, and yeast. It's possible that the only oats that were in the bread were the few grains sprinkled on top.

8

The Oat Bran Way

Oat bran, oat groats, and rolled oats can be used in an astonishingly wide array of recipes—from muffins and breads to stuffings and main dishes and vegetables. Experiment with oat products in your own kitchen. Oats add a sweet, nutlike taste to baked goods and casseroles and blend well with many ethnic dishes. Here are a few of the best oat recipes to get you started.

The Perfect Oat Bran Muffin

Yield: 12
Preparation time: 10 minutes
Baking time: 17 minutes

2¼	cups oat bran
¼	cup brown sugar or honey
1	tablespoon baking powder
½	teaspoon salt (optional)
1¼	cups skim milk
3	egg whites or 4 ounces egg substitute
1	tablespoon vegetable oil

1. Preheat oven to 425 degrees.
2. Lightly oil 12 medium-size muffin cups and dust with a little oat bran. Or line with paper baking cups, or use nonstick cups.
3. Combine dry ingredients—oat bran, sugar, baking powder, and salt—in a mixing bowl.
4. Add milk, eggs, and oil and mix just until dry ingredients are moistened.
5. Fill muffin cups with batter and bake in preheated 425-degree oven for 17 minutes, or until lightly browned.
6. Turn out onto wire rack to cool.
7. All muffins can be served hot or at room temperature.

Recipe can be doubled. Oat bran muffins do not rise very much so you can fill the muffin cups almost to the top. For lighter muffins, beat egg whites until stiff, then fold in at the end.

If muffins are not eaten within 24 hours, refrigerate or freeze. *To freeze:* Wrap muffins securely, store in freezer up to 3 months.

Variations: Many kinds of fruits and nuts can be added to oat bran muffins. The two basic additions are walnuts and/or raisins. Add ½ cup walnuts or ½ cup raisins, or ¼ of each for a crunchier, sweeter muffin.

Apple Oat Bran Muffins

Yield: 12 muffins
Preparation time: 10 minutes
Baking time: 20–25 minutes

1⅓	cups oat bran
1	cup rolled oats
¾	cup whole wheat flour
1	tablespoon baking powder
2	tablespoons brown sugar
1½	teaspoons cinnamon
2	egg whites
½	cup plus 2 tablespoons undiluted apple juice concentrate
½	cup plus 2 tablespoons water
¾	cup unsweetened applesauce
2	tablespoons vegetable oil
½	cup grated fresh apple with peel or chopped dried apples

1. Preheat oven to 400 degrees.
2. Lightly oil 12 muffin cups and dust with a little oat bran.
3. Combine dry ingredients—oat bran, oats, flour, baking powder, sugar, and cinnamon—in bowl and mix. For finer consistency, put dry ingredients into container of a food processor and blend.
4. In another bowl, whisk egg whites lightly and combine apple juice with water, applesauce, oil, and grated apples.
5. Combine apple mixture with oat mixture.
6. Divide mixture among 12 medium-size muffin cups.
7. Bake for 20 to 25 minutes, until tops are lightly browned.
8. Turn out onto wire rack to cool.

Raspberry-Banana Muffins

Yield: 12 muffins
Preparation time: 10 minutes
Baking time: 20 minutes

1 cup buttermilk
1 teaspoon baking powder
1 teaspoon salt
2 tablespoons vegetable oil
½ cup dark brown sugar, firmly packed
1 very ripe banana, mashed
1 pint fresh raspberries or 10 ounces frozen raspberries, thawed
4 egg whites
2 cups oat bran

1. Preheat oven to 400 degrees.
2. Lightly oil 12 muffin cups and dust with a little oat bran.
3. Blend buttermilk with baking powder. Allow to stand for 5 minutes.
4. To buttermilk mixture, add salt, vegetable oil, brown sugar, banana, and raspberries. Stir to blend well.
5. Whip egg whites until soft peaks form.
6. Fold buttermilk-raspberry mixture into egg whites.
7. Gently fold oat bran into raspberry mixture and mix until oat bran is just blended.
8. Divide the mixture among 12 medium-size muffin cups.
9. Bake for 20 minutes, until muffins are lightly browned and firm to the touch.
10. Allow to cool for 5 minutes before turning out onto wire rack.

Cranberry Muffins

Yield: 12 muffins
Preparation time: 10 minutes
Baking time: 20–25 minutes

½	cup uncooked fresh cranberries, rinsed and drained
¼	cup honey or maple syrup
1	tablespoon vegetable oil
1¼	cups skim milk
1	teaspoon orange peel, grated
1¼	cups oat bran
1¼	cups whole-wheat pastry flour
1	tablespoon baking powder

1. Preheat oven to 400 degrees.
2. Lightly oil 12 muffin cups and dust with a little oat bran.
3. Place cranberries, honey, oil, milk, and orange peel in blender and blend at medium speed for 30 seconds.
4. Add oat bran, flour, and baking powder to mixture and blend until just mixed.
5. Fill muffin cups with batter.
6. Bake for 20 to 25 minutes or until lightly browned.
7. Turn out onto wire rack to cool.

Zucchini Muffins

Yield: 18 muffins
Preparation time: 15 minutes
Baking time: 20–25 minutes

1	cup oat bran
1	cup whole-wheat flour
1	tablespoon baking powder
½	teaspoon salt (optional)
2	egg whites
1	cup skim milk
2	tablespoons vegetable oil
3	tablespoons fresh basil, minced
1	cup zucchini, grated
	Grated Parmesan cheese for garnish

1. Preheat oven to 400 degrees.
2. Lightly oil 18 muffin cups and dust with a little oat bran.
3. Combine oat bran, flour, baking powder, and salt in a large bowl.
4. In a separate bowl, beat egg whites; blend in milk, oil, basil, and zucchini.
5. Add zucchini mixture to flour mixture. Stir only until dry ingredients are moist; batter should be a little lumpy.
6. Fill muffin cups with batter and sprinkle with Parmesan cheese.
7. Bake for 20 to 25 minutes until lightly browned.
8. Turn out onto wire rack to cool.

Scottish Oatcakes

Yield: 32 cakes
Preparation time: 20 minutes
Baking time: 20–25 minutes

3	cups Scottish or Irish oats (steel-cut oats)
1	cup whole-wheat flour
¼	teaspoon salt
1	teaspoon baking soda
1	teaspoon brown sugar
4	tablespoons tub margarine
1	cup hot water

1. Preheat oven to 375 degrees.
2. Lightly coat two 10 × 15-inch baking sheets with vegetable oil.
3. Mix oats, flour, salt, baking soda, and sugar in a bowl.
4. Melt margarine in the hot water and gradually add to the dry ingredients. Mix well to form a dough.
5. Roll out to ¼ inch thick. With a cookie cutter or a heavy glass, cut into 3-inch circles and place on prepared baking sheets.
6. Bake for 20 to 25 minutes until lightly browned.
7. Cool on wire rack.

Buttermilk Biscuits

Yield: 12 biscuits
Preparation time: 5 minutes
Cooking time: 15 minutes

2	cups finely ground oat flour
1	tablespoon baking powder
¼	teaspoon salt (optional)
1	cup low-fat buttermilk

1. Preheat oven to 425 degrees.
2. Lightly oil a baking sheet.
3. Combine oat flour, baking powder, and salt in a mixing bowl.
4. Add buttermilk, and mix until just blended.
5. Drop batter by heaping spoonfuls onto prepared baking sheet.
6. Bake for 12 to 15 minutes or until lightly browned.

Oat Bran Bread

Yield: 2 loaves
Preparation time: 45 minutes (plus two hours rising time)
Baking time: 35 minutes

1	package active dry yeast (¼ ounce)
¼	cup warm water
¼	cup tub margarine
1	tablespoon brown sugar
1	teaspoon salt
2	cups scalded skim milk
2	cups oat bran, finely processed
4	cups sifted unbleached all-purpose flour

1. Preheat oven to 400 degrees.
2. Process oat bran in a blender or food processor until it is smooth and floury. Set aside.
3. In a small bowl, sprinkle yeast into water and stir gently once. Sprinkle a few grains of the salt on top. Set aside for about 10 to 15 minutes.
4. In the meantime, combine margarine, sugar, and salt in a large bowl. Add hot milk and mix. Cool to a lukewarm temperature.
5. Stir in yeast, add 1 cup oat bran and 1 cup flour. Mix well with a wooden spoon. Gradually add remaining bran and flour as you mix the dough.
6. Transfer to a floured work surface. Knead for 10 to 12 minutes or until smooth.
7. Wash and lightly oil the mixing bowl. Place dough in bowl, cover with plastic wrap or clean towel, and let rise until doubled in size, about 1½ hours.
8. Punch dough down and let rise for 30 minutes more.
9. Mold dough into 2 loaves and place in lightly oiled 9 × 5-inch loaf pans. Let rise again until doubled in size, about 45 minutes.
10. Bake loaves for 35 minutes or until lightly browned.
11. Cool in pans for 10 minutes. Turn out onto wire rack to finish cooling.

Oat Scones

Yield: 12 scones
Preparation time: 15 minutes
Baking time: 12–15 minutes

    1   cup Scottish or Irish oats (steel-cut oats)
    ¾   cup low-fat buttermilk, warmed
  1¼ cups whole-wheat pastry flour
    ½   cup oat flour
    1   teaspoon baking soda
    ¼   cup margarine, cold
    2   teaspoons additional oat flour

1. Preheat oven to 400 degrees.
2. Mix together oats and buttermilk in a small bowl. Let stand for 10 minutes.
3. Mix together whole-wheat flour, oat flour, and baking soda in a large bowl.
4. Cut margarine into flours with a pastry blender or a food processor until crumbly.
5. Add the oats and buttermilk mixture to the flours and mix well to form a dough.
6. Divide dough in half. Dust with oat flour, place on a lightly oiled baking sheet, and press into 2 patties, each about ½ inch thick.
7. Score each patty, cutting only partially into the dough, to form 6 wedges.
8. Bake for 12 to 15 minutes until lightly browned.
9. Cut pieces all the way through and serve hot.

Oats and Fruit Cold Cereal

Yield: Approximately 18 servings

1	cup oat bran
2	cups rolled oats
1½	cups toasted wheat germ
3	cups wheat bran or wheat flakes
1	cup chopped dried apricots
1	cup chopped walnuts
1	cup raisins
½	cup brown sugar (optional)

1. Mix all ingredients together in a bowl.
2. Keep refrigerated in airtight containers.
3. Eat as cold cereal.

Oat Bran Cereal

Yield: 2 servings
Cooking time: 2 minutes

⅔   cup oat bran
2   cups water
⅛   teaspoon salt (optional)

1. Combine oat bran, water, and salt in a saucepan. Mix well.
2. Bring to a boil over high heat; lower heat and simmer for 2 minutes, stirring once or twice.
3. Serve plain or with skim milk.

Creamy Oat Bran Cereal

Yield: 2 servings
Cooking time: 10 minutes

1	cup water
1	cup skim milk
⅛	teaspoon salt (optional)
½	cup oat bran

1. Bring water, milk, and salt to a boil in a saucepan.
2. Slowly sprinkle in oat bran while stirring. Reduce heat and simmer for 8–10 minutes, stirring occasionally to prevent sticking.

Crunchy Oat Bran Cereal

Yield: 2 servings
Cooking time: 15 minutes

1	cup skim milk
1	cup water
1/8	teaspoon salt (optional)
1/2	cup oat bran
1	teaspoon maple syrup
2	tablespoons oat groats, toasted

1. Bring milk, water, and salt to a boil in a sauce-pan.
2. Slowly sprinkle in oat bran. Reduce heat. Add maple syrup and simmer for 10 minutes.
3. Toast oat groats in a dry skillet or in the oven for 3 to 5 minutes
4. Stir into cooked oat bran and serve.

Rolled Oat Cereal

Yield: 2 servings
Cooking time: 3 minutes

½   cup rolled oats
1½ cups water
⅛   teaspoon salt (optional)

1. Bring oats, water, and salt to boil in a large saucepan.
2. Lower heat and simmer for 3 minutes.
3. Remove from heat, cover, and let stand for 12 to 15 minutes.
4. Serve with skim milk, and raisins, cinnamon, or bananas.

Creamy Rolled Oat Cereal

Yield: 2 servings
Cooking time: 10 minutes

  1 cup rolled oats
  1 cup water
  1 cup skim milk
  ⅛ teaspoon salt (optional)

1. Combine oats, water, milk, and salt in a large saucepan. Bring to a boil.
2. Reduce heat and simmer for 10 minutes, stirring occasionally.

Porridge

Yield: 2 servings
Cooking time: 25–30 minutes

2	cups water
1	cup Irish oatmeal or steel-cut oats
1/8	teaspoon salt

1. Bring water to boil in saucepan. Stir in oats and salt.
2. Reduce heat, cover pan, and simmer for 25 to 30 minutes, stirring occasionally.
3. Serve with skim milk, honey, or fresh buttermilk.

Oat Bran Pancakes

Yield: About 14 pancakes
Preparation time: 5 minutes
Cooking time: 5 minutes

1	cup oat bran
½	cup self-rising unbleached flour
2	teaspoons baking powder
1	tablespoon sugar
1½	cups low-fat buttermilk
2	tablespoons vegetable oil
3	egg whites

1. Mix ingredients together in a blender or beat with a whisk. Batter can be a little lumpy.
2. Pour batter by ¼ cups onto lightly greased hot griddle or skillet.
3. Serve with unsweetened fruit compotes, syrup, or honey.

Classic Oatmeal Cookies

Preparation time: 30 minutes
Baking time: 8—11 minutes

1¼	cups margarine
1¼	cups brown sugar or sugar substitute
2	egg whites
1	teaspoon vanilla
1½	cups unbleached all-purpose flour
1	teaspoon baking soda
1	teaspoon salt
1	teaspoon cinnamon
¼	teaspoon nutmeg
3	cups rolled oats, uncooked

1. Preheat oven to 375 degrees.
2. Beat together margarine and sugar until light and fluffy.
3. Beat in egg whites and vanilla.
4. Combine flour, baking soda, salt and spices.
5. Add to margarine mixture and mix well.
6. Stir in oats.
7. Drop by rounded tablespoonfuls onto ungreased cookie sheet.
8. Bake 8 to 9 minutes for a chewy cookie (10 to 11 minutes for a crisp cookie).
9. Cool 1 minute on cookie sheet.
10. Remove to wire cooling rack.
11. Store in tightly covered container.

For variations: add 1 cup raisins or chopped nuts.

Creamy Zucchini Soup

Yield: 4 servings
Preparation time: 15 minutes
Cooking time: 30 minutes

1	tablespoon olive oil or margarine
1	onion, finely chopped
⅓	cup oat bran
⅛	teaspoon black pepper
2	cups chicken broth
2	cups zucchini, thinly sliced
1½	cups skim milk
1	tablespoon fresh parsley, minced
⅛	teaspoon white pepper
⅛	teaspoon dried thyme
2	scallions or fresh mint, chopped, for garnish

1. Melt margarine in a medium-sized saucepan and sauté onion until soft.
2. Stir in oat bran and black pepper. Add chicken broth slowly, stirring constantly.
3. Bring to a boil, lower heat, cover, and simmer for 30 minutes.
4. In a separate saucepan, steam zucchini, or cook with a little water and then drain, for 5 minutes, until tender but still green.
5. Add milk to zucchini and in a food processor puree until smooth. Return to saucepan.
6. Let oat-broth mixture cool slightly, then pour into blender or food processor and blend for 1 minute.
7. Add zucchini puree and blend for 15 seconds. *Note:* Using a blender will give the soup a frothier consistency than the processor.
8. Reheat soup to desired temperature and season with parsley, white pepper, and thyme. Garnish with scallions or mint. (Add more milk or broth if soup is too thick.)

Hearty Mixed Vegetable Soup

Yield: 6 servings
Preparation time: 15 minutes
Cooking time: 30 minutes

5½ cups chicken broth
2 cups carrots, peeled and sliced
1 stalk celery, sliced
2 cups broccoli, chopped
½ cup onion, finely chopped
1 teaspoon dried tarragon
½ teaspoon salt (optional)
¼ teaspoon black pepper
½ cup oat bran
1½ cups skinless chicken breasts, cooked and chopped

1. Combine broth, carrots, celery, broccoli, onion, tarragon, salt, and pepper in large stock pot.
2. Bring to a boil; reduce heat and simmer, covered, for 15 minutes.
3. Stir in oat bran, and simmer gently for 10 minutes, stirring once or twice.
4. Add cooked chicken, and continue cooking until chicken is heated through. Serve piping hot.

Minestrone

Yield: 12 servings
Preparation time: 30 minutes
Cooking time: 1 hour, 15 minutes

1	cup whole oat groats, rinsed and drained
½	teaspoon salt (optional)
3	cups water
2	tablespoons olive oil
1	clove garlic, minced
1	medium onion, chopped
½	head small cabbage, chopped
3	stalks celery, chopped
2	carrots, peeled and chopped
4	cups canned tomatoes
¼	cup oat bran
1	teaspoon each, dried oregano, thyme, basil
1	cup fresh or frozen lima beans
1	cup fresh or frozen cut green beans
1	cup cooked pinto or kidney beans
5–6	cups water or chicken broth
¼	cup chopped fresh parsley
	Grated Parmesan cheese for garnish

1. In a saucepan combine oat groats, salt, and 3 cups water and simmer, covered, for 40 minutes.
2. Heat oil in a large soup pot and sauté garlic and onion for 1 minute.
3. Add cabbage, celery, and carrots. Sauté 1 to 2 minutes.
4. Stir in tomatoes, oat bran, and herbs. Simmer, covered, until vegetables are tender, about 20 minutes.
5. Add lima beans, green beans, pinto beans, cooked oat groats, and 5 to 6 cups of water.
6. Simmer until beans are tender.
7. Add parsley and continue cooking for one minute.
8. Serve hot with grated Parmesan cheese for garnish.

Old-fashioned Oat Stuffing

Yield: 4 cups
Preparation time: 30 minutes

Oat bran, oat groats, oat bread, rolled oats can all be used in stuffings. Experiment with your favorite stuffings and dressings for poultry, fish, veal, or pork. Whatever recipe you're using, remember to add a little additional liquid to accommodate the extra absorbency of the oats.

1	tablespoon margarine
1	tablespoon olive oil
2	stalks celery, chopped
1	onion, chopped
	Giblets from turkey or chicken, chopped into small pieces
1	cup cooked oat groats or cooked oat bran
2	cups dry whole-wheat or dry oat bread in small cubes
1	teaspoon each, dried thyme, tarragon, sage, and marjoram
¼	teaspoon salt (optional)
¼	teaspoon black pepper
½	cup water or chicken broth

1. Melt margarine and olive oil together in skillet.
2. Add celery and onion and sauté for 3 minutes.
3. Add giblets and continue to simmer until giblets are cooked through.
4. In a large mixing bowl combine oat groats and bread cubes with herbs, salt, and pepper.
5. Add giblet mixture to oat mixture and mix.
6. Add water to stuffing to moisten. If stuffing seems dry, add a little more liquid.
7. Stuff dressing lightly into neck and chest cavities.
8. Follow roasting instructions.

Pureed Cauliflower

Yield: 4 servings
Preparation time: 12 minutes
Cooking time: 8 minutes

Cauliflower pureed in a blender looks and tastes like mashed potatoes. The addition of oat bran turns this simple dish into a significant source of soluble fiber.

- ¾ cup water
- 4 cups cauliflower, chopped
- ⅛ teaspoon salt (optional)
- ¾ cup oat bran
- 1 tablespoon tub margarine
- ¼ teaspoon white pepper

1. Boil water in a large saucepan and add salt. Add cauliflower and cover. Reduce heat and simmer for about 8 minutes, until cauliflower is tender.
2. In a blender or food processor, blend in small batches cauliflower, cooking water, pepper, and oat bran until smooth.
3. Transfer to serving bowl and serve hot. Puree can be reheated if it has cooled during the processing.

Note: Blending in a blender give purees a lighter, airier texture than processing in a food processor. Purees can be made with almost any vegetable. Carrots, turnips, or broccoli all make excellent purees.

Whole Oat Pilaf with Wild Mushrooms

Yield: 4 servings
Preparation time: 10 minutes
Cooking time: About 50 minutes

1	cup oat groats, washed and drained
1	tablespoon vegetable oil
1	medium onion, finely chopped
1	ounce dried wild mushrooms, sliced (reconstituted*)
1/3	pound domestic fresh mushrooms, sliced
2	cups chicken broth
1/4	teaspoon ground black pepper
3	tablespoons fresh parsley, minced

1. Sauté groats in vegetable oil for 3 to 4 minutes.
2. Add onions and continue to sauté for 3 more minutes.
3. Add wild and domestic mushrooms and sauté 5 more minutes.
4. Add broth and pepper and bring to a boil.
5. Reduce heat and cover. Simmer for 40 minutes, stirring occasionally, until liquid is absorbed. If pilaf becomes too dry during cooking, add 1/4 to 1/2 cup of water. Check pilaf after 35 minutes. If it is too wet, cook last five minutes with cover off.
6. Remove from heat and stir in minced parsley.

*To reconstitute dried mushrooms, first rinse thoroughly under cold running water. Then soak in water, broth, or a little wine until softened. Mushrooms can then be sautéed in margarine to bring out their full flavor before adding to the dish, or added directly.

Whole Oat "Rice"

Yield: 4 servings
Preparation time: 5 minutes

1	cup oat groats, rinsed and drained
¼	cup chopped onion
1	tablespoon olive oil or margarine
2	cups chicken broth

1. Sauté onions in olive oil until translucent.
2. Add broth and bring to a boil.
3. Add groats. Reduce heat and simmer for 40 minutes, until liquid is absorbed.

Savory Eggplant, Pepper, and Zucchini Casserole

Yield: 4 servings
Preparation time: 20 minutes
Cooking time: 60 minutes

½	cup oat bran
½	teaspoon oregano
½	teaspoon basil
¼	teaspoon black pepper
¼	teaspoon salt
1	medium-size eggplant, sliced lengthwise into ¼-inch-wide slabs
5	medium-size zucchini, sliced lengthwise into ¼-inch-wide whole lengths
1	can whole tomatoes, mashed
1	large Spanish onion, thinly sliced
2	sweet red peppers, seeded and sliced

1. Preheat oven to 350 degrees.
2. Lightly oil casserole dish.
3. Mix oat bran, oregano, basil, pepper, and salt together.
4. Build one layer of vegetables—eggplant, zucchini, tomatoes, onion, and red pepper—and spread oat bran mixture over it.
5. Continue layering vegetables and oat bran until all ingredients are used. End with oat bran mixture on top.
6. Cover and bake for 45 minutes.
7. Uncover and continue baking for 15 minutes longer or until top is brown.

Salmon Croquettes

Yield: 6 cakes
Preparation time: 15 minutes
Cooking time: About 10 minutes

1	can (8 ounces) red salmon
3	egg whites
½	cup oat bran
½	cup celery, finely chopped
½	cup onion, finely chopped
1	tablespoon lemon juice
1	tablespoon skim milk
3	tablespoons olive oil

1. Combine salmon, egg whites, oat bran, celery, onions, lemon juice, and milk in a bowl and mix well.
2. Shape into 6 cakes.
3. Heat oil in skillet and sauté cakes until well browned, about 5 minutes on each side.

Oven Baked Fish

Yield: 6 servings
Preparation time: 15 minutes
Baking time: 25 minutes

    3   tablespoons vegetable oil or margarine
    ¾   cup oat bran
    ½   teaspoon dill
    ¼   teaspoon ground black pepper
    3   pounds fish fillets
    2   egg whites, beaten
    ¼   cup skim milk
    1   lemon, sliced

1. Preheat oven to 375 degrees.
2. Coat bottom of shallow roasting pan with vegetable oil.
3. Combine oat bran, dill, and pepper in a shallow bowl.
4. Blend skim milk into egg whites
5. Dip fish into bran mixture, then into egg mixture, then into bran mixture again.
6. Place fish in roasting pan and bake for 10 minutes. Turn and continue baking 15 minutes, until second side is lightly browned.
7. Serve garnished with lemon slices.

Hot Spicy Oven Fried Chicken

Yield: 6 servings
Cooking time: 30–35 minutes

¾   cup oat bran
½   teaspoon each, dried basil, tarragon, and thyme
¼   teaspoon paprika
¼   teaspoon cayenne pepper
⅛   teaspoon black pepper
⅛   teaspoon salt
3   whole chicken breasts, split, skin removed

1. Preheat oven to 400 degrees.
2. Place all the dry ingredients in a shallow dish and mix well.
3. Rinse chicken in cold water and drain. Leave slightly wet.
4. Coat each piece completely in bran mixture.
5. Arrange chicken in a shallow baking dish, meaty side down. Bake for 15 minutes. Turn chicken and bake another 15 to 20 minutes, until brown.*

*If chicken thighs or legs are used, increase baking time to a total of 40 to 45 minutes.

Classic Meat Loaf

Yield: 6 servings
Preparation time: 20 minutes
Baking time: 60 minutes

Rolled oats or oat bran can be added to your favorite meat loaf recipe. The following recipe uses a combination of both.

1	pound lean ground beef
1	pound ground veal
1	large onion, finely chopped
1	stalk celery, finely chopped
2	teaspoons fresh parsley, minced
1	teaspoon each, dried tarragon and thyme
¼	teaspoon ground black pepper
2	egg whites, beaten
1	cup rolled oats
½	cup oat bran
⅔	cup broth or skim milk
1	cup tomato sauce or canned whole tomatoes, mashed

1. Preheat oven to 350 degrees.
2. Mix all ingredients except tomato sauce in a large bowl.
3. Pat meat loaf mixture into a 9 × 5-inch loaf pan.
4. Bake for 30 minutes.
5. Pour tomato sauce over meat loaf and return to oven. Continue baking for another 30 minutes or until top is brown and meat loaf is slightly pulled away from the sides of the pan.
6. Let stand for 10 minutes before serving.

Afterword

What is on the horizon for the future protection of our hearts? Health research daily continues to point out new connections between nutrition and good health, and everyone should stay alert for new developments.

Food manufacturers may be able to create margarines and shortenings rich in stearic acid, the one fatty acid which doesn't appear to increase cholesterol. Even better, cattle breeders and ranchers may eventually hit on a way of raising animals that are high in the good saturated fat and low in the bad.

Other techniques to lower fat and cholesterol levels in milk, eggs, and other animal products may be developed.

Cattle and pork industry executives believe that they will be able to develop leaner animals. New biological technologies, such as using growth hormones to alter metabolism of animals to develop leaner meat, is one method. A similar and less expensive method is to keep cattle on the range longer and in the feed yard—where they fatten on grain—for shorter lengths of time.

Also under development from two different manufacturers is a low-calorie, cholesterol-free substitute for fat. The FDA has not yet approved the new fat substitutes for safe use in humans, but if the new products are eventually approved they are expected to have wide use both as an addition in prepared foods and in cooking oils and shortenings. The fat substitutes are expected to be used in such products as french fries, ice cream, salad dressing, mayonnaise, yogurt, butter, and cheese spreads.

Pharmaceutical companies are also contributing to the growing store of knowledge about cholesterol and heart disease. As scientists seek new drugs to reduce blood cholesterol in high risk people who do not respond to alteration in diet, they have discovered much new information about the complex mechanisms that control cholesterol in the body.

All of these new discoveries, ideas, and potential food products reflect a trend in personal health management that experts anticipate could lower the incidence of heart disease in America by one-third over the next twenty years.

If you begin a cholesterol-lowering diet today featuring oat bran, how long will you personally have to wait? The most immediate results will probably be seen in triglyceride levels, which may actually start going down within hours. Eat less fat and cholesterol today, and have better triglyceride levels tonight. Your total cholesterol level takes a little longer, but the latest research says that reducing fats and cholesterol in your diet can bring improvement in three to eight weeks.